Thorns in My Quilt

Letters from a Daughter to Her Father

Mohua Chinappa

RUPA

Published by
Rupa Publications India Pvt. Ltd 2024
7/16, Ansari Road, Daryaganj
New Delhi 110002

Sales centres:
Bengaluru Chennai
Hyderabad Jaipur Kathmandu
Kolkata Mumbai Prayagraj

P-ISBN: 978-93-6156-627-1
E-ISBN: 978-93-6156-456-7

First impression 2024

10 9 8 7 6 5 4 3 2 1

Printed in India

To
fathers and daughters
daughters who become mothers to their fathers
daughters who wish they were heard more…

Contents

PREFACE

These are letters written to my Baba. I know it is merely a monologue as I will never receive a reply.

I have made peace with his silence.

I started writing these letters to ask the questions I wanted to ask him before he passed away in August 2022.

I had to muster courage—to be vulnerable requires strength. So I delved into my past.

To the world, Baba was well-read, well-travelled and a handsome man. But he was also a man who didn't hesitate to hurt his daughter, even at a tender age, with his words, which cut through my heart, each and every time!

Baba was not expressive when it came to praise or appreciation. It left me questioning myself and my worth. Only to realize, albeit much too late in life, that he was projecting his fear and anger onto me.

There was an abundance of resentment, temper and criticism towards most things I did or chose in life. This, in turn, shaped me to be obedient and subservient. It is this kind of upbringing that makes girls like me remain chained to our circumstances.

Over the years, like a sinister shadow, I measured my self-worth through my father's eyes and it governed my reactions to the world, especially around men.

I hope this book will help readers who want to conquer the struggle against the 'why me?' syndrome and learn how to deal with the lack of love from parents, the love that children ought to receive unconditionally. I was there and figured the way out and so can you.

I finally understood this indifference he had shown towards me and how it was in complete contrast to some rare and great moments of tenderness and love.

But he was a wonderful grandfather to my son, Neel, and I am grateful for that.

These letters are not only about questions that remained unanswered but also about telling him how Ma and I picked up the threads of our lives after his passing. Writing these letters has been a roller coaster of emotions.

I hope this book is for everyone trying to survive the loss of a parent and the burden of being born a girl.

I think there is immense power we can derive from opening up our hearts to people around us. Similarly, the power the other person derives when we open up to someone is no less potent. I hope my letters help you find what you are looking for.

Mohua Chinappa
Bengaluru

Family, Friends and More...

My father, Bidhu Bhushan Bhattacharjee. He is no more, but always around. He lives on in my spirit, constantly urging me to question all that is unfair in my world.

Baba's story is ordinary—but full of extraordinary moments of learning and unlearning. He will live forever in my heart and soul.

I pictured myself on the creaking see-saw that I sat on, week after week, in a dialysis unit. As I fell, my side hit the floor with a thud, hurting my spine and legs. I watched Baba deteriorate. He kept oscillating between the conscious and the subconscious—the world he was slowly sliding into. He was losing his mind to dementia and was unable to speak coherently or read, two things about him that I always took for granted.

During my numerous visits to the hospital with him, I watched the degeneration of his extremely intelligent mind. His frail body was slowly poisoning itself; the mind could no longer distinguish between reality and the unreal.

In his extreme pain, all he wanted me to do was comfort him. But my Baba was dying, and I was helpless.

I watched the red blood passing through the machine and being chased up through the vent on his thin arms. I wept as I recalled the same arms in a chequered tweed coat in the winter of Shillong as I walked with him, holding his finger, certain that those strong and reliable arms would always be there for me. How wrong I was!

Baba was the quintessential Bengali—opinionated, emotional and embarrassingly honest, especially about his bowel movements. He was a family man and loved his wife intensely.

He loved to have coffee and cake with me in cafés. On the occasional lunch dates, we used to order a glass of wine, and he would urge me not to mention it to my mother. I obediently didn't.

He doted on my son, Neel. All he wanted was to talk to his grandson every day. He wanted to hear his voice and get to know him just a little bit more. He knew my son better than I did, he would say, and I basked in this indulgence.

Baba had an insatiable wanderlust. He wanted to discover new cultures, visit historical places and buy books from each place he visited. He loved to talk about cinema, books, art, photography and world history. He debated the actions of world leaders and their inhumanity. He was raised in a left-leaning family, and steadfastly held on to that ideology.

Baba was among 11 children brought up in an educated East Bengal family. His father, my late grandfather, Jamini Kumar Bhattacharjee, was an upright and honest man, a gold medallist from Dhaka University. The family left their ancestral home before partition as my Thakurda found a job in Shillong. My Thamma was the only daughter of her established family in Comilla, Bangladesh. Thamma delivered all her 11 children in her parents' home, which had a temple, a big pond with numerous fishes and a bustling atmosphere, providing constant care and comfort.

Shillong was a small village until 1864 when it became the new civil station of the Khasi and Jaintia Hills. It remained the summer capital of East Bengal and Assam for many years. Consequently, one can find a large population of Bengalis in the hill state, which seems to be a remnant of India's colonial past.

But like many displaced Bengalis, they lived fragmented lives. Baba, lovingly called Chandan by his family and friends, yearned for his home till his last days, even as he pursued financial growth and security for his family. In the bargain, he lost his health and his mind.

He kept telling me that they had found radium in his blood. 'Report this,' he would tell me, for radium could be sold at a premium price. I would always nod and agree with him. I failed to understand why, even in his disturbed mental state, all he wanted was to be financially secure.

As I grew older, our roles reversed—I became his mother. But I am grateful that I had the opportunity to play the role—a relationship that he may have missed in his own childhood.

I grew up overnight with his passing. As his ashes floated away in a terracotta urn into a place unknown, I prayed he wouldn't bump into the rocks and boulders on the swirling river. His journey into the afterlife should be smooth.

My mother, Rekha Bhattacharjee. She was born in Faridpur, in undivided Bengal. Just before Partition, her parents moved to Delhi with her and her younger brother.

She is cosmopolitan, yet remains partial towards everything that is Bengali. Ma wore Bengal cotton saris in Delhi's summer months and pure silk saris in winter. But now, she is unrecognizable. She no longer takes pride in her appearance. She is in her nightdress all day, crouching in a corner of her room, or curled up in bed, wondering at the unfairness of death, that it claimed her husband before her. She was sure she'd go before him.

Ma has been in deep grief—clinically depressed—after losing Baba. She used to be a good writer and painter and created such beautiful things by hand. From dolls made from orange squash bottles to crocheting doilies and helping me with stitching homework for my convent school, Ma did them all. She loved to stitch my dresses as well, following designs from Western catalogues. She would oil and braid my hair every night.

Ma was a working woman, feisty and financially independent. She faced the insurgency in Shillong and our subsequent move to Delhi, where she seamlessly fit in, being fluent in Hindi, having grown up in the city, and with the support of her extended family.

Ma used to have a girl gang at her Shillong office. They had tea parties and the occasional movie evenings. She never seemed lonely, despite the fact that my father was often out at work. She always found a way to live her life, with me in tow.

But Ma was also short-tempered, even harsh on occasion.

I took care not to anger her as a child. But there was an unspoken camaraderie that I shared with her, something that was almost sisterly. She knew most of my secrets, except those that she couldn't prise out of me.

She shared a love–hate relationship with Baba and used to complain about his discerning taste for good food (which made him something of a critic) and fondness for fried items. It seems to me that her life revolved around cribbing about my Baba, coupled with an incessant need to please him.

Once a social being, Ma has not made friends in the many years that she has been living in Bengaluru. She clings to me, convinced that I will fill her lonely evenings. I try not to let her down.

Ritualistic and traditional, she prays every morning and night. But she keeps to herself and has little emotion to spare for others unless they are closely related. Called Jhuru di by her cousins, her world now is limited to her four walls, and an occasional visit to the temple or a cousin's home.

Ma doesn't wish to travel. Neither does she want to come out of her bedroom, not even to go to the park outside. Sometimes she stands by the gate, a small figure in her nightdress, peeping through the grille at the world outside.

Neel, my loving son. He is my only child—and the light of our collective lives.

He is the reason why I look forward to a new day every day. I have felt joy, watching him grow—from the little baby he once was to the sensitive adult he now is. He completes my life with his sheer presence. My Baba seldom smiled but always had a smile for Neel—a smile that came from his heart, achingly beautiful and pure.

Chinappa, Chini. He is the man I grew up with.

We met when we were in our early 20s. After two years of writing letters, magical moments and wonderful dates, we got married, against his parents' wishes.

After 24 years of marriage, moving cities, becoming parents, and many memories—mostly happy, while some extremely painful—we decided to separate in 2020.

In the deepest recesses of my heart, I am still trying to hold on to the fun years of togetherness before they ebb away. Because of our shared past, he will remain the person I hope to reach out to in my unfamiliar life in Bengaluru at 2 a.m. I hope he will pick up the phone if I call, and that's a testament to the family I tried to create here.

Shimonti Sinha. She is my artistic school friend. A Bengali, she and I bonded over our Delhi upbringing and common roots.

Ashu Kainth. My childhood friend based out of Leicester, UK, has taken every call of mine during these tumultuous years and listened to me without judgement and only love. Her voice soothed me on days when it seemed there was no light at the end of the tunnel.

Asif Jukaku. He is my colleague, a friend who has seen me through the different stages of my life—as a family person, a grieving daughter and as a rebooter.

Shanti. She is my colleague who has secured a place in my heart effortlessly.

Raj. My father's nurse was a good cook, a safe driver and affectionate towards me. The role Raj played during Baba's illness kept me going. Every time I recall Baba's last days, I see Raj trying to feed him and clean him up.

Mahesh. He is my cook, or rather, my confidant, and Raj's brother. He tells me about everyone at home when no one is looking or listening. From Ma, he has learnt how to prepare *sukto*, *potol paturi*, *posto bata*, and other Bengali delicacies.

Hussain. He is my driver, a Sylheti Bengali from Agartala. Like many Bengalis, he was looking for a home in Bengaluru where his inherent need for a post-rice siesta would be understood. He found that with me.

Zarina. She is my house help, a Bodo Christian girl from Assam. She is somewhat moody, extremely trustworthy and loves fashion. She lost her mother as a young girl and then moved from one house to another to find a place where she would get a hearty non-vegetarian meal every day. Zarina must have at least one egg with her two meals and is happiest when she is promoted to the post of household monitor. With her honesty and straightforwardness, she has carved a place for herself in my heart.

They are my family.

LOSS

4 August 2022

Living Room, Bengaluru

Dear Baba,

Today is your s*hraddho*, the puja for your departed soul. Referring to you as a soul seems so distant. Calling you anything but 'Baba' seems like two strangers speaking to one another.

The *purohit* is here to do the rituals. The atmosphere is sedate. The room is lit and the flowers in the vases are in full bloom.

I am glad we have cousins in the city; otherwise, it would be very lonely for Ma and me. We know very few people who would make the effort to attend a staid function like a shraddho. How does one end a tie so deep with a mere ritual? One can't.

It does feel surreal to watch your photograph with a jasmine garland around the lifeless frame. The sandalwood *phonta* or *tika* on your forehead makes you look different. The living room has been cleared. The large antique box has been covered with a white cloth, and your photograph is placed on it in such a way that you are facing the direction that will lead you to the other world.

The shraddho among Bengali Hindus is a ceremony that is performed to ensure a passage for the recently deceased to the other world. The rite is both social and religious and is meant to be conducted by the son. But you have no male heir. So I defy tradition and lead the puja.

I follow the rites dutifully and chant the mantras, which don't mean much to me. You are gone. There is no mantra that can soothe my heart. On the floor is a bed, laid out with a pillow and an umbrella for your onward journey to God-knows-where. I follow the purohit. Neel joins me in the ceremony. I feel so anchored, having him next to me. What a loving child he is. He makes life so much simpler for me.

After the puja, we put out a plate of your favourite food so that a crow can come and eat it. Leaving the food in the corner of a lane seems ridiculous, but I have decided not to question any of the rituals, for I don't want Ma to feel that I didn't do my best.

I leave the plate on the ground. There are bottles strewn around, and the ground is not very clean. I don't turn back for another look.

Your photo has now been removed and stands on my marble corner table. I put out the burning incense sticks and remove the flower garlands. It is still sinking in that I won't be able to hear your voice ever again, calling out to me, asking me for something or the other.

As we sit down to eat, Neel reminds me how you discussed Left politics and he argued with you on capitalism, just to rile you up in jest. You had such a wonderful bond with my child.

I smile as I hear Neel mimic you and your quintessential Bengali ways of reacting to situations. Those debates between you both. I loved the way you both called each other Dadu. Baba would say, 'Dadu, you must read about the world and its magnificent history. The great idea of how civilizations emerged, and how revolutions took place in protest against tyranny and oppression. As you read, you will learn that the world is a beautiful study of humanity and historical events.'

And Neel would say, 'Na, Dadu, I will only read books that emphasize the profit and loss of capitalist businesses. Whoever cares about art and philosophy?'

Neel knew how you would go red in the face. And you would say, 'No businessman ever built a nation; it is the thinkers and the dreamers who created a world of equal opportunities.'

This camaraderie you both shared remains the most beautifully preserved and poignantly pure memory of you with your grandson.

I remember those days when you constantly waited to hear from Neel, and how the Sundays were marked aside to have your long-awaited conversations with him.

You truly were a wonderful grandfather to my son.

I feel empty as the furniture in the living room is rearranged to how it was before. Like nothing has happened, and no one is now gone forever. It looks as if you will come back in a minute, ask for a cup of tea and brood with your arms crossed over your chest. I think just being there to watch me do everyday things made you feel calmer. I don't know. But I hope someday, I will understand the silence between us. Comfortable spells of silence, and some very terrifying ones. Like your death.

Love,
Manu

5 August 2022

Bengaluru

Dear Baba,

The vermilion has been removed now.
The parting is stark white
the hair oiled
tied into a braid
of acceptance.
The grey mixed with the leftover black strands
falling carelessly
on her shoulder.

I had seen her
one lonely noon
take a pair of scissors
cut off her locks
Like Samson and Delilah.

She was at war
A war with her own existence
Her identity has been shaken
Her oar is cracking open
along with her broken sail.

She sets to the seas
but
the land is far away on the horizon
shining like the crystals

found on a crown
lost in a war
lying forlorn
for the head of the right king
but now Samson is dead
the Philistines have left too
the palace has been torn down
but parts are intact.

Her locks sheared
from guilt
for being alive.

Will she find her shore
with her broken boat
and tattered sail
hoping
the seas take her in
or the fire of her breath
is gutted before it becomes wild
like a forest fire
burning the little birds
coloured kites stuck between branches
and her capsizing boat too
lost
in the new world!

Love,
Manu

7 August 2022

Bedroom, Bengaluru

Dear Baba,

I am reminiscing about our days in Shillong, where you're holding my little hand as we walk down a hilly road. The weather is crisp, the sky so blue that it's almost turquoise. Butterflies flutter around the blue hydrangeas. I trip along, jumping over the clear little water puddles.

The Kongs*, with their chequered shawls, huddled under a big black umbrella, sell sour berries. As we walk on, we pass the little chapel of your college, St Edmund's. Your voice comes to me like an echo: 'Father Canning told me that I must pursue literature.' You look so satiated with life. I feel happy to be walking with you, hand in hand.

As we, father and his little daughter, walk down, I—as I am now—climb up a hill.

My view is different from up there. The climb is arduous, with sharp little rocks jutting out of nowhere, as though they want to cut and bruise my feet. My knees hurt. My heart is shattered. I want to hold on to the younger me, holding your hand. I want to frolic in the soft green bed of grass covered with yellow and white wildflowers. But I can't reach out.

Here I am, watching us both, but unable to touch them. I watch helplessly at us, walking and looking so

*Kong means sister in the Khasi language.

free and full of love.

I know I can't feel those fingers grasping my hand. I remember your wrinkled hands, your last touch, and how your fingers encircled mine, with hope.

I can hear the doctor say, 'Call a GP and have him declared dead. Get the death certificate.' I sobbed and said, 'He is warm, still warm!'

The little girl traipses by with her father. It is such a picture-perfect image of warm security. But it can't be touched or experienced—only imagined.

My body heaved with sobs as I slowly felt you going cold. Like ice.

If we could only pass each other again. We would hold hands, laugh out loud and be kind. I know you will hold my hand, the way you did to help me down the steep slopes of rain-drenched Shillong.

Love,
Manu

8 September 2022

Bengaluru

Dear Baba,

Ma walks into your room without acknowledging your bed. She refuses to look at the place where you breathed your last. It pains her.

Ma is a shadow of herself now—frail and resigned. I think she misses being your wife. She feels bereft.

I can't look at her as a widow. Thankfully, she seems distant from the rules that so many women have to follow as widows.

Her cheeks hang, laden with strong sad lines. Her eyes are lowered and in constant thought. She is restless and it feels like she needs to reach a place but can't just yet.

As I write, I can recall with absolute clarity the way you gasped for breath and then your eyes rolled up, and you stopped breathing. Your body was warm even after your heart stopped beating. Ma was silent. She asked Shimonti quite calmly to bring some *Gangajal* and to put it in your mouth.* I still don't know how it went down your throat. The water didn't dribble out. You were silent, just like the way you had become. You had been extremely quiet for days. As the caregiver turned you on your side, I saw your

---

*In Hinduism, during the final rites, Gangajal is poured into the mouth of the deceased, which is thought to help the soul attain satisfaction and quench its thirst.

tongue roll out of the side of your mouth. It reminded me of a game you played with me when I was a child.

You would fake death by putting your tongue out, and I used to frantically push you, force you to laugh and call me a fool. The game ended even before it began.

I also saw the large red sores on your back. They had been there for long. You had lost speech and none of us knew.

The room on 1 August was filled with people. But only Ma and I were together in our loss. We looked at each other. She just sat on a chair and said, 'He is gone!'

I refused to believe it and, as always, wanted to take you to the hospital, just once. Just once again, to revive you and hold on to the threads of life, maybe jumbled up, but still lit with the warmth of the beating heart.

I had an anchor in you. Or was it the other way around? Whichever way, we were a family. Suddenly I felt cold. Your head and feet were turning cold too. Your face became yellow. The dark pall of grey had lifted, replaced by a jaundiced yellow.

The sanitized room, with Ma sitting on a chair with everyone around her, was like a page out of a story I had read before. Ma resembled a leaf, found fluttering in the desert storm, a leaf trying to hold on to the shifting sands. Desolation enveloped her like a cloak of fatigue.

She held out her palm and watched her lifeline. I knew the question in her heart: for how long was she going to live?

I know for sure that she wishes she were no more. You both were a unit. As the years passed, you both bonded even more in your lonesome life in Bengaluru. This was never home. It didn't have the fragrance of the *shiuli* flower blossom during Durga Puja, nor did it have your acceptance or love. You both just followed me to this city. You were so dependent—and so isolated.

Ma wants to charge your mobile phone. It is as if you are going to get calls. She has kept the phone on a shelf. I don't touch it. It frightens me that if I do, I will break down emotionally, knowing that those fingers won't ever dial me again.

Like Ma, I too sit, awaiting a final answer from the mountain that I have built with all the sharp little stones of resentment, guilt and anger collected over the years.

Ma wants you to reach out to her and hold her finger. Your Moni, as you lovingly called her, misses you. I couldn't see this love bond or trauma bond between you and Ma when you were together. There were only a few moments of tenderness. I remember instead the constant conflicts between the two of you.

But you were her purpose. Her undying habit was having you; that was her life.

I wish I could hear from you.

Love,
Manu

13 August 2022

Bengaluru

Dear Baba,

I can see you sitting on a chair on my veranda. The barber has been called to cut your hair, shave your beard, trim your nails and massage your head.

You look like a little boy—in a red sweater and a pair of track pants, feet placed firmly on the ground. As I go closer to say hello, your face twists into a shape that is unrecognizable. You start hurling words at me, calling me names. You are spewing hatred.

I remember your face and the words so well. '*Oshikkhito borbor*,' you screamed, 'uneducated savage!'

I feel anger rise up in me. My first reaction is to fight back and ask you to shut up. But I am embarrassed to be shouted at in front of the barber. Your caregiver looks at me as if I am a clown. I clench my jaws and laugh, pretending it's all a joke. They join in my little pity party. They laugh, but hesitatingly.

Your eyes are full of rage. It's like if you had the power, you would kill me with your words.

I walk inside the house. I can hear the doctor telling me, 'He is losing his mind. Dementia is setting in.' I am ashamed of my anger towards you. I steady myself and walk towards the refrigerator. I take a slice of cheese and stuff it down my throat. The cold cheese gives me warmth.

As I eat, I feel calm. I decide to go back to where you

are sitting. You see me and start hurling hurtful words again. This time I don't laugh. I stand still and say, 'Yes, you are right about everything you say.'

You calm down and your face now no longer shows disgust. Instead, you look defeated.

I watch you cry and shrink and my innards tighten. I tear up, as if cut by the shards of a broken mirror. It is so badly broken that it can no longer hold a reflection and has mixed with the gravel of time. The only remnant is the twinkle of a glass that held the reflection of a small and happy family in Shillong, many years ago. But to me, it's like a mirage. Did it even exist?

Love,
Manu

15 August 2022

Bengaluru

Dear Baba,

Since your passing, I often wonder what dragged me down into this sinking feeling of helplessness, where I feel out of place in the world I inhabit.

I am insecure about losing my mother. There will be no one then to anchor me. I struggle in the darkness with no light ahead.

What happened to the little girl who ran behind butterflies in Shillong? Believed that rainbows beamed across the sky when jackals got married? What happened to the girl captivated by the aroma of bakeries and the picture of moss growing on walls?

I feel totally devastated. Deep grief shakes you to the core. You begin to question yourself and walk down a slippery slope. I have no interest in my own passions—or in anything at all.

In my next life, I want to be born without any awareness or intelligence. It's so much easier to live in the dark; the only light you follow is the glitzy one of bars and roads.

It's a curse to be a woman. And, more so, an intelligent one.

I feel so lost.

Love,

Manu

26 August 2022

Bengaluru

Dear Baba,

Ma sits alone, slouched on the red chair on which you sat and got riled with me. I walked into the dining area today and found her dark face hanging, half in shame and half in fear. Have you ever seen a face like that? A face that shows years of being abused for being a daughter, a working wife and a mother to a daughter?

I got frightened seeing Ma sleeping on your chair, her mouth half open, breathing in little snores, legs apart. She looked like a small man. She doesn't wear her saris any more. She is always in a nightie, with a thermal, a blouse and a sweater. It's an ugly nightie. I don't see her doing *shringar* any more. She has no interest in dressing up or looking beautiful like she did in the past.

You used to buy her such beautiful saris, so tasteful and stylish, when you travelled. In Delhi's summer, she used rice water to starch her cotton saris. It seems like a thing of the past, a life that was a dream—of cotton saris in summer, and silk in winter. Where did the beautiful woman, your wife, go?

How can a widow feel so empty? So bereft, consumed by an all-encompassing sadness?

I wonder how you would have reacted if Ma had left you a widower. I think you would be more devastated than she is now. I think men find it difficult to pull themselves together when their wives go before them.

Men are lousy as widowers! And this is despite the fact that society never asks them to give up non-vegetarian food, wear white or mourn till they are alive. But a man usually dies a bitter death without his spouse. There is no one to fuss over him the way his wife did. No one to cook food the way he likes it, brew the tea to suit his taste. She is the maid with the golden touch, who can satisfy her husband's whims and fancies.

What would you have done if Ma had gone before you?

Love,
Manu

1 October 2022

Bengaluru

Dear Baba,

When I think of what women have to undergo as widows, Dida and Thamma come to mind. They ate fish all their lives but gave it up after the passing of Dadu and Thakurda. They had to wear white till they died, and were forbidden to do even rudimentary shringar. They had to pray they would never be tempted to ever look at another man with lust or desire. Did they ever feel desire? How did they process temptation?

Ma was very embarrassed one day when we were going to a Durga Puja pandal. She plucked out the bindi from her forehead, and said, 'What will people think?' I asked her, 'Which people?' 'People at the puja,' she replied. I said, 'Don't worry, no one will have the guts to say anything to your face. If they say anything, it would be behind your back—and you should have no issues with that.'

I put the bindi back on her forehead. She looked quite sweet. Small and bony, with sunken cheeks, my little girl, my Ma, with the bindi on her forehead.

Do I see myself in Ma?

I see myself in mourning, but not in the extreme way she does. I don't have to give up non-vegetarian food. I especially love fish cooked with florets of the winter cauliflower, in a light gravy infused with black cumin seeds. It reminds me of Shillong winters. The fresh fish and the tasty *jhol* that Ma used to make. My cook has now learnt to prepare the curry like her. He cooks it with equal love for me. It tastes as good as Ma's.

Why should I give up my dietary habits, my attire, if I were to be in a situation like Ma's?

I wonder if you would want your wife to do that. Or me.

You told me how well your mother cooked. Ma had learnt from her a coriander chutney prepared with garlic, green chillies, roasted black cumin seeds and a dollop of mustard oil. It had to be eaten with hot rice. My mouth is watering as I write to you.

You loved food—but perhaps more than the taste you enjoyed the control you had over it. As one ages, one loses one's sense of self-importance. I saw you diminish as you grew older—you were angry and almost contemptuous of me many times. There were more moments of disgust than love.

But food was always obedient to you. You could control the portion, the taste and the lull you received from a dish. But one day you got over that too. As your body got sick, your taste buds vanished. The best biryani or the best food couldn't help you heal. You searched for the freshwater fish from Bengal and the greens that grew by the ponds in the villages and towns of eastern India. Is this what happens to most of us in life? Do we search for lost tastes, hidden lanes, aromas of childhood bakeries and the sun with a happy face?

Love,
Manu

2 October 2022

Bengaluru

Dear Baba,

Goddess Durga is here. Preparations for prayers and festivity have begun. It feels strange not having you in our plans for pandal visits or seeing you in the family photo we clicked together every Pujo. You came mainly for the *bhog** and the fare at the food stalls that we enjoyed together. The stalls were not there for the last Pujo during the Covid-19 pandemic. I remember how you sat in the sun after eating the bhog, looking so effortlessly handsome.

For me, I was just happy to dress up in a sari and match with Ma. You loved running to the Bengali bookstalls, searching for new Pujo book releases, which you collected and read with such pleasure. When Neel was around, your joy doubled. Everything was all about what Dadu wanted. He would tease you, and you would gently rebuke him, saying, 'Dadu, don't say that!'

I remember the joy on your face as you watched me eat *shorshe bhapa ilish*—hilsa fish steamed with a paste of mustard seeds in a banana leaf. You used to love watching me eat, and was gleeful when I took a piece from your plate and ate it.

---

*In Hinduism, bhog refers to food that is served for free to all those who come for the Puja. The most common form of bhog is the khichdi, served with a semi-dry vegetable preparation, sweet tomato chutney and payesh, which is a rice pudding.

This Pujo, Ma feels alone. We didn't buy a sari for her. She was in no mood to go to the pandals but finally agreed after a lot of persuasion.

I was thrilled that she had agreed to go out with me. As I came down, I saw that she had dressed up. Ma looked nice. As I complimented her, she looked at me tentatively, so unlike her previous self. Then, as I wrote in my last letter to you, she removed the red bindi from her forehead. 'I can't be seen with a bindi. I am a widow now!'

I couldn't believe my ears. I pulled myself together, and then I put the bindi back on her forehead.

Ma has lost 10 kilograms since your passing. She looks small and frail but once in a while, I get a glimpse of the Ma my heart remembers.

We walked to the pandal. Music blared as I took her towards the idol. For the first time, she had no interest in the rituals. She blocked her ears with her hands and said she was going to collapse.

I was stricken and angry with myself for making her leave home. She needed more time to seek closure after the death of her husband.

Somehow, we managed to bring her a chair so that she could sit. Finally, our car drove up, and I ushered her into it. That was the end of Ma's Durga Pujo.

Pujo won't be the same for me either. With you gone, the connection to my culture, which includes this major festival, has come to an end.

I must learn to live with memories of the Shillong Pujo. It was small but we had so much fun. Then came Delhi, the government house with the *tulsi* (basil) plant in the backyard, and the shiuli that blossomed and spread its fragrance during the Pujo season. Now I am in Bengaluru, a member of a group that has easy access to bhog. But the shiuli calls me and urges me to go back to another time.

I miss you, Baba!

Love,
Manu

15 October 2022

Bengaluru,
Window seat at Blue Tokai Coffee Roasters

Dear Baba,

When I sit down in a café, ready to write, I sometimes wonder where I learnt to write. I don't know how it happened, but writing came to me like a lover on a lonesome journey, an arduous path through steep hills.

I look at the rain-drenched streets of Bengaluru. The trees are dripping, the flaming orange flowers seemingly paying obeisance to the grey skies above.

Why do I travel every time it rains to a place outside the present? I now find myself in Shillong. The rain, oh, the beautiful rains of the happy place we left behind!

I don't know why I remember those days. It may be the constant rain or the dripping umbrella opposite me. I travel back in my mind with the umbrella, onto the roads of Shillong.

The damn black ubiquitous umbrella has no idea of the emotion it draws out of me, the strength it has over my heart. I long for the days of simplicity amid the hills that had secrets and stories.

Love,
Manu

16 October 2022

Bengaluru

Dear Baba,

It is raining again. The rain takes me to the cold, wet days of Shillong. I am sitting in Bengaluru, transported to a place that holds those memories. I remember the butter cookies you made, and the aroma of vanilla essence in our little dark kitchen. It filled up my nostrils as you let me take a sniff from the newly opened bottle. Memories can be so weird.

I can still see that little bottle of vanilla essence, with its red tin cap. You poured a few drops into the batter. The blue oven—a little box with a glass door—worked on electricity. We watched the batter fluff up with heat in the oval biscuit mould tray. It went up and then down, like the waves of my heart. Those were such wonderful days!

I also remember our holiday in Puri. The hotel room had a large veranda. I recall watching the waves ahead. I had a fever as usual. You were with Ma, standing on the shore of the sea. The shore always reminds me of an infiniteness that I crave. But life has different pathways for us all. Each time I recall the emotional security I had with you both, I feel a devastation that seems almost unbearable. I can watch my body being swept ashore by the angry waves. But they won't consume me, however much I wish they would, ending this battle of trying to find a space in this vast world.

When I look back, I feel like a splinter in my glass house. The glass house is in little bits. Some bits are piercing my heart, some are in the balls of my feet. I hide the bloodstains as I walk into the darkness of my heart. The laughter and giggles fade behind me. I pick up the broken shards of glass so that Ma won't find them out.

Do you remember those days of my childhood? I had a constant fever and an odd sensation I could never describe. I sometimes felt I could see the three of us, deserted, in a separate universe, crying out in pain to come together and be at peace.

Love,
Manu

20 October 2022

Bengaluru

Dear Baba,

It's early morning now. Ma has woken up and I can hear her footsteps on the stairs. She holds on to the railings, fearful of missing a step. I pray that she takes care.

It poured last evening. I sat in the living room. There was beauty all around me. But I felt disconnected from everything, including Ma. She sits still, looking at the floor. It looks like she is grieving so much that even her eyelids are tired and heavy, and can't be raised. She stares intently at the floor as if looking for answers.

Is she seeking answers to the eternal question of how to cope with life without a spouse? Or wondering what would happen to a man who'd lost his wife?

Men of your generation and mine were not encouraged to express their emotions. So they learnt to internalize pain, sorrow and deep grief. The only expression allowed was a bit of happiness that was demonstrated in a rare hug given to the wife near other family members. In many cases, a physical relationship between a mother and a father was almost unthinkable. So the emotions are all inside. This kind of conditioning becomes even more scary as the man grows older and lives without his spouse.

In most relationships, the wife takes on the role of the mother and the man remains the child. An older man living alone is a frightening thought. Such men tend to give up their battle against a terminal illness once their spouse has died. Sometimes, they find themselves among children who resent them. Where do such men go?

Have you found a home? Is there love in it?

Love,
Manu

25 October 2022

Bengaluru

Dear Baba,

A few days ago, I found that Ma had woken up early. The morning light fell on the papers. Ma stood there, by your bedroom doorway, wearing your red sweater. In that light, the red looked as if she had smeared herself in blood.

She said, 'Look at me!'

Ma looked broken, almost crazed. Her grey hair had got mussed up when she pulled the sweater over her head. With her eyes staring into mine, she said, 'This sweater will keep me warm this winter.'

I blurted out, 'This is Baba's! It's too big for you.'

She said, 'It's okay on me, it's not big!'

I was speechless. I think it was for the first time in her life, in my memory, that she had chosen to wear red. Ma used to be so elegant, always draped in white, beige, blue or lilac.

She stood against the doorway like a haunted doll, the red sweater hanging from her wrinkled, bony body, her nightdress peeping out from underneath. This picture will remain etched in my heart forever. Fortunately, I was able to convince her to wear a thermal under her nightdress. The thermal is white. I wish you were here to see her.

Love,

Manu

20 December 2022

Bengaluru

Dear Baba,

It is winter now. When it rains in December in Bengaluru, you know how it gets just a bit cold. For Ma, though, it's too cold. What's strange about the city this year is that the rain-drenched leaves and the mud all around aren't romantic at all. It seems soaked in sadness. This weather is depressing. It appears as if it's seeking revenge, trying to bring us all to our knees, for all our wrongdoings.

But today, for a change, God let the sun come out from behind the clouds for a while. It appeared like a tiny sliver of hope in the debris of death around me, like a little burst of happiness. I feel my mood lift as the sun casts its warm shadow over my cold and damp heart.

I watch Ma's tiny body at the dining table; she is reading a newspaper. She no longer reads the zodiac columns. When she was married and her life was full, she would read the zodiac forecasts in *The Times of India*. I used to trust those forecasts. Those days were strangely warm in the government quarters of New Delhi.

We knew our neighbours, and they knew us. The women exchanged little bowls of special food. The neighbour's dish became the dish of the day at home for us. I recall the *rajma* that came in a steel bowl with a lid. Sometimes, we received potato gravy with *vadi*.* Ma used to return the plate and bowl with something special too—it was an unwritten rule to never send back an empty bowl.

Now she is surrounded by all kinds of luxuries, but seemingly living in deprivation—her bowl is empty, and she is alone. When she tries to tell me something, it's always depressing. She mentioned that as she stood at the gate a few days ago, she waved to the lady whose house is opposite ours. Ma raised her hand and said, 'Me, Rekha!' 'The lady,' Ma said, 'replied, "I am Krishnamani".' And then she smiled and went back inside.

Ma often stands forlorn at the gate. She hopes to make a friend, but the 'connect' is missing. I know she can no longer find it. I hear the longing in her voice when she makes a call to our relatives in Delhi every evening. I can hear her sobbing to her yoga teacher. Yes, she now has a yoga teacher.

When she wakes up every morning, she walks gingerly down the stairs or sits reading the local news in the newspaper. I feel relieved—for my sake and hers—that she has survived another night of being a widow. Widowhood is like a shroud of death. You live every day like a punishment, reminded that you are no longer needed by anyone.

I carry on. I get hassled and am tired most days. But today I have picked up some force from the sun. I search for Ma. I find her at the spot where the sunlight is stronger. A white shining car is parked there. On the side of the bonnet is her red-and-white chequered handloom towel. I get irritated.

---

*Both are Indian delicacies.

'Why is the towel on the car?' I ask her. She replies, 'I find it difficult to climb up to the terrace and put it out to dry.'

I say, 'Let me do it for you.'

She replies, 'No, I will take it off the car soon. I promise.'

I feel ashamed asking her about the towel, making her conscious of her little middle-class ways, which are mine, too. But I have travelled further away from the place I used to call home. Ma has, too, but she feels defeated. She is different from the Ma I knew as a child. She was feisty, angry and mean.

Ma also has a way of making others feel sad for her. She is supremely intelligent, too.

Ma holds a mirror to widowhood in India, but I thank her stars that she didn't suffer the way her mother did. Unwanted, my grandmother died alone after a cardiac arrest in her fourth-floor Delhi apartment. There was no one to dab her lips with water or put a tulsi leaf in her mouth in her last moments.

The silence of the widows across India is deafeningly loud. I can hear them chant into eternity. Yet they die in indignity, alone, unwanted and in chaos. The widows beg in Vrindavan. All because they are no longer married, no longer someone's wife. A widow loses her sense of self. I realize that Ma's temper, her ego and haughtiness, came from the support she had from you. You were loyal to her. You had decided to stay married in disharmony.

I tell her it's okay for the towel to dry on the car, but she continues to be apologetic. She stands there in the sun with her shoulder-length hair, oiled and grey. She looks haunted. Her eyes look larger than before against her sunken cheeks. An image comes to my mind: she has the look of a lost fawn in a forest that is on fire. The flames envelop every inch around her but spare her. Even though she seems to want the flames to consume her, her punishment is being alive. But the flames don't touch her. She stands in solitude.

It is already four months since you left us. I don't allow any memory of yours to become too real, lest it reach my heart. Those memories are like a dam—the water on the other side threatens to burst out, but the stoic dam keeps up the façade of harmony.

My heart feels like a hollow vessel flowing away in the Kaveri River. I can hear the sound of the gurgling water; I am one with the bobbing vessel.

I still recall watching a twig dip in and out of the moving waves of the river. I wondered where would your *asthi*—ashes—travel. Which soul would you meet? All I pray is you find the love that you never had. That was the reason for your anger and constant criticism. I wish I could meet you just once again; hear you once, just once again.

Love,
Manu

7 January 2023

Bengaluru

Dear Baba,

Ma sits at the dining table, unshed tears in her eyes. Her face has shrunk, and the skin sags around her cheeks. The light from the window shines on her, like the light of divinity. It cascades all around her but does not fall on her. She sits like a ragged doll, her tears as lost as she is.

She mutters, 'I wonder where all the people have gone.'

I ask her, 'Who are you referring to? Baba?'

She replies, 'No, everyone.'

I say, 'I too keep thinking where Baba is now…if he is coming back soon.'

She looks away and raises her bony hand to dismiss the conversation.

She refuses to acknowledge your absence. An intense pain burns deep within her. She is miserable without you.

Yesterday, she asked me, 'Shon, listen, almonds are good for your health, nah?'

I nodded.

She said, 'What is the point… Eventually, all of us have to leave. It's going to be sooner and not later. What's the point of eating almonds?'

I said, 'Look, you are alive and you must continue to live as you have. This is how it is!' I felt cruel saying this to her because I know, for her, this means a punishment. To live life is an ordeal for her.

Slowly, she goes towards the gate and half opens it to watch people on the streets. From her demeanour, I know she feels like a destitute. There is nothing around her she can relate to—neither the Kannada signage nor the people and their culture. I wonder if she wants to see the street as her outside world and then again return to her cocoon inside my home, with me. She refuses to go anywhere any more.

I watch her objectively. I can see a frail woman of 45 kilograms in a nightdress. She wears a thermal and a sweater in temperate Bengaluru and still feels utterly cold, with frozen emotions. I want to touch her. But I don't want to break her reverie of finding herself out of her cage. She is like those birds that don't chirp with the morning sun, but scatter grains around their little cages and you will see how they find their tunes—with chains tied around their feet—birds that are kept in cages, and feel secure without a glimpse of the open sky above.

I must admit that I can relate to her search for you. I keep wondering where you are now. Ma says the soul lives forever. The *atma* is immortal. But how do I find you? Where do I search for you?

I do see you in so many things around me and feel your absence. But I can't fathom Ma's loss even now.

Ma comes back to the room, back from the gate, and says that the Bangladeshi girl, who was your neighbour in Bengaluru, had called.

I don't believe her; I feel she must have made that call herself. Apparently, she told Ma that everyone was picking the squash from your garden and the sandalwood tree was dry with no one watering it.

So I promised to go next week and have a look at your house. I haven't been able to pull myself together to go there yet.

As I write, I can see your bustling home. The dining table, always with food in steel vessels, your book, your hearing aid, your spectacles, your chair with the backrest, the *ponjika*—the Hindu almanac, the little plastic bowl with cut fruit and *nokuldana*[*] that Ma offers to the Gods every morning. The house has life and love. It has Bengali books and an old tape recorder and cassettes.

I know I will shatter into smithereens when I open the door and enter your home.

Nowadays, Ma uses many of your things. She was scratching her back with your steel backscratcher, the one like an elongated fork with blunt ends. I asked her, 'This is Baba's! Where did he buy it from?'

She replied, 'Yes, it's his. I have no idea where he got this from.'

I would have felt guilty using the scratcher on my back. It would have felt as if I had no reverence for your belongings. We have given away most of your things—barring some old files and your wallet with an ATM card that said B.B. Bhattacharjee.

I touched those letters as gently as I could. It was like caressing you. The sadness I feel is incomprehensible. The card can't understand my bond with those letters; the name that I said aloud to others with pride and a sense of belonging.

---

[*]Nokuldana, also called Nakul Dana, Ram Dana and Mimosa sugar balls, is a popular prasad in India.

When will we three meet again?

Will it be on the shores of Puri, or the boat on the Mekong River, taking us to Laos? Or maybe in Bengaluru? The three of us lost will find our way back together to our home.

Love,
Manu

15 January 2023

Bengaluru

Dear Baba,

The sunlight crept in from the left corner of the door left slightly ajar. Sharp and visceral, it danced around in circles, like dervishes lost in their inner world. The cobwebs knew that this space where they had been hanging precariously for a while now, and enjoying the sunlight, was temporary. They were as temporary as everything and everyone else in the room.

The cutwork sheer white curtain dropped. It seemed to have merged with the bedspread and the cloth that had wrapped up my Baba.

The rainwater had seeped into the walls. The peeling paint on the sides was like surreal art. Dali in the hanging clock and on the wall paint. The broken cement had mixed with the chipped paint, forming bubbles.

The bubbles were full. They resembled your hope of living life, of going back to your place of belonging. What is this sense of belonging? I often ask myself. Have I ever belonged to anyone? Even if it was for a few days or minutes? Did I feel totally in sync with the universal desire for belonging?

Did I ever find that oasis of love, gentleness or that complete absence of insecurity and fear with my husband, my parents, my child? Strewn around lost hopes and my shattered being? Was belonging like a glass full of water on a summer afternoon? I see the glass with a sliver of a crack, the water slowly dripping from it. The water resembled a placid lake trying to find its flow.

It takes me back to the memories that you shared with me—as a young college boy at St Edmund's. Good-looking, well-read and deeply unhappy. I imagine watching you walk around the lake. The ducks paddled, swooping into the water, raising their head and shaking off the excess water.

Can human beings do that too? Shake off the excesses that we carry all our lives?

Love,
Manu

16 January 2023

Bengaluru

Dear Baba,

Illness does break one's spirit. One starts to pray and seek mercy from God to be able to heal. I saw you reading the Gita, with the sacred thread around your shoulder and arm that you had never worn before. I wonder if you were regretting being a rebel, or was that the last hope you were holding on to—the hope that God would give you a lease of good health and a better life.

I see myself lying on the bed next to you. We face each other, teardrops falling down the side of our cheeks, soaking the pillows. We both know our minds are connected with the collective pain of our unmet dreams—and the torture of not being able to ease our individual pain.

My body is wracked by an autoimmune disease. I try to raise my hand above my head, but can't raise it beyond the elbow. My legs are swollen and the toes are tightening like a noose. My eyes hurt as I stare at the light entering the room. It touches my retina and it pokes like hundreds of needles all at once. The pain is unbearable. The acceptance that I may never heal makes me weep.

As I turn my gaze away from the light entering through the window, I look up and find a little blackbird sitting on the blades of the unmoving fan. The bird doesn't want to fly out.

You don't look up.

Your left arm is thinner than before. Your body quivers with pain from time to time. It has sketch-pen marks to identify the spots where a vent will be inserted to clean your failing kidney. You don't move as you know there is no return. The diaper packets are piled up on one side, the oxygen cylinder is in another corner. I try to speak, but my throat is dry. 'How are you?' I manage to ask you.

'I am doing okay,' you reply softly.

I wonder what gives you the strength to say that you are okay. I don't know if I ever will be like you. I want to tell you that I don't have your courage. But all I say is, 'That is good. You are feeling well.'

We can't turn our bodies, so we stay on one side and look at each other. The light of the day changes; it is now dusk.

The blackbird has flown away too. It fluttered its wings and went out into oblivion.

With the evening light, I can see there are butterflies around our heads, dancing in circles. The caterpillars can't move; they have fallen around the pillows. The beauty of the butterflies overshadows the death lurking around us.

Tears continue to stream down; now the sides of our faces and our hairs are wet. For you, these are tears of resignation; for me, the tears hold hope of a new life, of making myself stronger from the crisis and joining the dance of love with the butterflies. Our love is so palpable, yet so restrained.

Your silence carries years of anger, resentment and pent-up rage. Words fail us both today. But I do want you to apologize to me for all your harshness. Just for this closure, I wait.

Speak up, Baba, speak up, please, if only today.

Love,
Manu

1 May 2023

Bengaluru

Dear Baba,

Ma is unable to pull herself out of her loss and anguish. This morning, as I went down to see her, I found her in bed. I touched her, and her bones pierced my body. She was so small that I felt I was holding a little girl. Her eyes welled up. She cupped my face, and said, 'Mamon!'

My mind went back to the lost sounds of the kitchen in our Delhi home—Ma cooking, the clanking of steel vessels. The sound seemed hollow today. Ma looked like she was bobbing in the ocean of sorrow.

I held her gently and urged her to rest. We hugged each other. She held on to me—as if she wanted to apologize for what she had become. My heart wept, but I was exhausted too, I wanted to say, caught in a web of her constant need for my presence and strength. But I smiled instead.

How does one seek an apology from one's own? We are supposed to accept our people with their flaws and their flourish, as we do with our own selves. So I promised her that I would always be by her side; I would not leave her. She said, 'I know.' Then she shut her eyes and tried to sleep. I watched her eyelids, heavy with grief, insecurity and fear.

My mind began wandering, taking an absurd turn. Do I need to prepare myself to face life as an orphan? How will I accept this life of loneliness without Ma?

No one ever taught us to let things go, or how to

process the death of a loved one. After all, death is the ultimate end to life's challenges that we face day in and day out. I feel Ma's umbilical cord is still attached to me. We are both entangled in our grief—both facing loss.

She was a very young mother—beautiful, artistic, strong, well-dressed and well-read. Who is this woman staring back at me? Empty, and broken from within?

She is unrecognizable. Her face is skeletal, and her eyes have lost their light. I can't reason with her mind, which is in the dark, unfathomable waters of despair. In this darkness, she is surrounded by her imaginary sharks and piranhas. But there are also a few blue dolphins; there is hope. I can see that her mind is raging. She falters as she tries to reach the shore and the deep darkness of her mind pulls her back into its abyss.

She feels so guilty to be alive. I doubt if anyone can ever imagine her feeling of waiting to go, to be with Baba.

Every night, she keeps a photo of a god on a plastic chair next to her bed, like a blanket of reassurance. On the opposite end is the bed where Baba breathed his last. I tell her to sleep upstairs but she won't. I think she speaks to him in her silence.

I want to throw her a net in her brooding ocean, to help her sleep, but she won't take help. So I mumble, 'Hold on, everything will be okay,' and she swims further away from me.

How do I process the diminishing of the strong, dominating mother that I knew, the one with an immense vigour for life?

How do I accept that her eyes will never light up the

way they did when she saw me all dressed up and ready to step out? Just her words—'You look beautiful'—brought a spring to my step. That look of absolute adoration was like a rock in my stormy ocean.

Ma couldn't turn her face away from me. She stared vacantly at me.

I feel lost. I don't know whom to call out to when my head throbs or my tooth aches. There will be no one to hear my cries, except for the skies above and an empty chair that they once took turns to sit on, with a cup of tea and a newspaper.

Tell me what to do, Baba.

Love,
Manu

SEARCH FOR ANSWERS

28 January 2023

Bengaluru Airport en route to the
Hyderabad Literature Festival

Dear Baba,

There is divinity in suffering and let me find that from here onwards.

I have been thinking about marriage and women. The only thing personal in a wife's life is her husband. The rest is public.

A woman loses her identity when she gets married. Her surname changes and, automatically, her identity is lost, as her life becomes intertwined with her husband's. She becomes part of a family and the honour and responsibility of this new space falls on her shoulders. She is now in the public eye—for how many children she bears, the gender of her children, and more. Her approval in the family circle is graded by her culinary skills, the home she manages, and how she forgoes her past identity for the new life that her parents have chosen for her.

She is judged for every line she has toed, every mistake she has made. Her menstrual cycle dictates when she can enter the kitchen and when she has to be confined to her room. The public scrutiny of her character is based on how happy her in-laws are. Her life is her husband's life. As they say, 'Pati Parmeshwar'—the husband is akin to God!

Love,
Manu

Dear Baba,

Where did love vanish? Why did it even appear if it had to be so fleeting? Such stingy little moments of joy—and then a dingy darkness all around. In that darkness one tries to hold on to the idea of love, never quite finding an answer.

So today I wish to write to you about love—the most beautiful feeling in the world. I guess love exists, but I am not certain if it really is there. More important, does it last till you die?

You found questions on love banal and were uncomfortable to have a conversation about it. But it was a feeling you searched for, and yearned for in your relationships your whole life. But the 'man' in you didn't wish to address this topic. You were full of anguish. I recall how you wept after every session of dialysis, and said, 'No one loves me.' It saddened me, but annoyed me, too. Why couldn't you see that there was love, in abundance? When I tried to hold you, not let you slip away, that was love. I do regret that I didn't hold your hand enough to comfort you. As always, I was worried about rejection; my ego came in the way. Yes, I failed to let you know that I loved you so much.

But like you, I don't know of love between man and woman, or father and daughter, and I am surprised when I hear stories of such love. The only love that I experienced was between Neel and me. It was—and is—all-encompassing for me. Most others were transactional. My love for my son and the love I received from him saved me from the great heartaches and mental breakdowns that I experienced with others.

All of us seek love that's forever; no one foresees endings. The toughest part of everything is the ending. So it's easier to not look at the end. 'What next?' is a difficult question for a couple, a parent or even friends. Friendships that end, parent–child relationships that turn ugly, are not spoken of. So we continue with the bitterness, the rejections and the dreary habit of familiarity.

When we start any relationship—or even a new job, for that matter—we walk into it with the hope of a 'forever'. Till we grow and find that our paths don't align, our destinations change. Like a train journey, when a station comes, people leave with their baggage and memories. In a close relationship, when the love ends, it slowly starts to melt like a burnt-out candle, the embers flickering in the darkness. And then, with one soft touch, the candle stub falls off the edges, forming a waxy white blob.

I collect the melted wax and hope to mould it back to its earlier shape. But it can't be done.

I must admit that I love the idea of a 'forever'. For work, for friendship, for love, especially for love. This—a man falling in love with a woman and a woman finding her fulfilment in her relationship—is like a dream. A dream made of puffy clouds, stardust and moonlight. It always evaded me, perhaps because, like you, I yearned for it too much. So love decided to touch my cheeks—like a warm summer breeze on arid land—and softened the parts that had dried up inside me. But it didn't last.

I look back at my love for Chini. It was so childlike when I met him. I had heard of Coorg (also known as Kodagu) but it didn't evoke much sentiment in me. What mattered to me were the letters he wrote and the flowers he gave me when we dated. I had never felt more physically beautiful. He would call me *chaykarti*, which means beautiful in Kodava Takk, the dialect spoken in Coorg.

I felt beautiful. We also looked good together.

Slowly, as the letters grew in pages, our longing too grew. We wanted to be together, so we spoke of getting married. I was fascinated by the idea of marrying into another culture and merging mine with it. I thought too ahead, perhaps. The courtship was unscathed till the marriage conversation with his family began.

They didn't want a Bengali daughter-in-law. They wanted someone from their own region. I found it difficult to understand why. I belong to an upper caste, majority community. I didn't understand this rejection. I was not raised to be insecure about losing my culture or identity, so I couldn't fathom this fear of someone from another community or region. I had grown up in Delhi, which had people from everywhere—my best friends were from Punjab, Rajasthan, Kashmir and elsewhere. We mingled effortlessly and took part in each other's important occasions and life events. So what was the big fuss?

After two years of dates, letters and happy moments, I was thrown into a wedding hall. His family members were angry that I was not the bride they wanted. They publicly disowned us.

I shudder to think how you must have felt to be screamed at, in a wedding hall full of people, by my late father-in-law, who said he didn't accept the marriage. I was quiet, and recall how you and Ma stood there, half ashamed, half embarrassed, for the wedding photographs. I am sorry you and Ma had to go through this for my sake. I wish I had foreseen this. That evening we couldn't speak but you told me to come back unhesitatingly if I felt small or disrespected. I often felt disrespected and was rudely spoken to. But I was young, too naive to question why I took this sort of mistreatment.

The memories stay within me, and they will remain forever. We never spoke about it, but we three knew it was humiliating and disrespectful.

I was losing my sense of self. As I grew, year on year, I also realized our life goals were different. But I had got used to the comfort of having tea together on weekends, he and I reading the newspapers. Anything outside this seemed frighteningly unfamiliar. But I also felt unheard and unseen. When I was being treated for an autoimmune disorder, I would go by myself to the hospital, year after year. Uveitis caused my pupils to dilate, and made me miss steps; I held on to strangers who helped me navigate to my car.

I thought I was unloved—and unlovable. For most, marriage becomes a comforting habit, with the two partners living in their individual worlds. We were in our own worlds too, and our worlds came together when Neel came into our lives. He brought us togetherness and immense joy, erasing all other feelings.

I think I stayed on only because I was a homemaker,

and had no income of my own. But when Neel left India, I was desperate to realign my life. I was frightened of what lay ahead. My heart was full of unspoken hurt, the dismissal and the lack of acknowledgement of my being. Many marriages go through this, but not many people have the courage to break free. We carry on, bitter together, or simply tired.

There were things that I never told you, things that hurt me immensely. I felt I couldn't breathe any longer and needed a future where I could honour myself.

So finally, one day, our marriage collapsed like a house of cards. I knew it was the end. We decided to live apart.

The weekends were lonely and I kept falling back into the habit of meeting Chini, and then feeling further unseen and more distraught than ever. I know my decision to separate angered you and Ma. Mainly Ma. I realized how traditional she was in her thinking, so rooted in the idea of marriage. It didn't matter whether it was good or bad. What mattered was that her daughter should not be tagged as a single woman or a divorcee. It was like a blot on her reputation and her standing in the extended family.

But after 24 years, I just couldn't stay in this marriage any more. The dam had burst, and I had to swim up to the surface.

It's been years since then. I am slowly settling into my lonely life in Bengaluru.

But I feel free in my loneliness. I don't feel the pressure to accept the disrespect that many women comply with. They, like me, wanted love but didn't quite understand respect. I woke up from my slumber and realized I wanted respect over anything else.

As homemakers, we give up economic freedoms and identities, hinging our lives with the homes we make. I carried on my back the decision to separate like a crazed woman. I broke down and cried near strangers or in familiar places, in memory of the harshness I had endured.

Once again, the *dkhar*—the outsider in Shillong—came dancing with its ghastly eerie steps. I was called the *borejathi,* the outsider in Coorg as well. At every wedding I attended, I was told how their boys and girls were not encouraged to marry 'outsiders'. I gulped down my emotions, and sometimes apologized or smiled.

I have much to write about—my loneliness, and my slow understanding that I needed a space where I could be heard, seen, understood and respected. I was done with this constant need to explain how I felt.

I now need to grow spiritually, away from attachments, including the one with you, and take my work forward. This place—inhabited by all of you—wouldn't allow me this. You were all selfish and wanted me at your beck and call. But no one was there for me when I called.

Grief has many layers to it. Betrayal from all of you gutted me.

Neel remains my hero on the ship that I am on, a ship with no sail.

In this tumultuous journey, my broken boat has a glass floor. I can see the corals, the coloured fishes, the clear water. I know that the oar is far away and that I may drown, but I know, even if I am drowning, I won't try and come ashore to the same place. As with these misadventures, in this lifetime I have seen marine creatures—just like angels—brush past me, reminding me of the bountiful nature of the ocean. There is an unending abyss, no doubt, but there is also the astounding beauty that I wouldn't ever experience if I didn't get into the boat of uncertainty without my oars and safety jacket.

Love,
Manu

PS: I am on antidepressants and sleeping pills to reduce anxiety, but I'll take this any day over that.

1 February 2023

Bengaluru

Dear Baba,

Things have not been easy. Chini is busy with work, and I have been trying to figure out what went wrong between us. When did he stop seeing how I felt and thought?

I recall when I started dating him, and the letters and the roses. And the promises—all broken, one by one. Did we break them together, or were they always meant to be broken so I could emerge from them?

How is it that you never found any fault in him? You pined to meet him and waited eagerly for those Sunday meetings. Was the fact that you lacked a son so intrinsically carved into your heart?

I remember how you walked all the way from your home to mine. I would peep out, and find you sitting at the dining table, arms crossed over your chest, a little plastic packet with a dish that Ma had made for Chini and me. Neel was studying abroad.

You spoke in English with Chini and with me in Bengali. I wonder now why it was so important for you to meet him for advice. You did that once a week!

You were intelligent in my eyes and knew it was I who did most things at home. Yet you sought advice from him, ignoring the fact that he had little interest in household matters, least of all yours.

But you continued, always hopeful.

I have to understand that I can't ask questions that need answers. So I keep falling back into the loop of why, how and why me?

Chini is angry with me, and has stopped communicating; we communicate one-on-one with Neel.

How could you both love him so much? Knowing he was withholding the respect and love I so craved from only him?

Maybe you never loved me. It is daunting to accept I was not loved for who I was, but for what I could do for you.

I can't stay quiet any longer. It burns me and angers me. I feel like the paper that I used to burn in the Shillong sun with glass. You keep holding the glass at an angle from the sun, watch the paper turn black and then crinkle, crumble and turn into ash.

I feel like that paper, and I am pained to know that I am unloved in the ways I perceive love to be.

This truth is always tough. What was my fault? Was it because you didn't see me suffer like you did? Or was it because you just disliked me?

I must come to terms with this open-ended conversation that my heart will carry with me forever.

I recall only a few tender moments that we shared. I hold on to those to remain alive and sane.

Love,
Manu

1 September 2022

Bengaluru

Dear Baba,

I achingly seek reasons for your anger towards me. I can't forget the night you told Ma, 'I am scared of Manu!' I can't get that out of my system.

There were some days when you deliberately wanted to hurt me. Do you remember when you said you would not give me a penny; that I didn't deserve anything?

Why did you dismiss me?

Was it because I was a girl? Was it because I became your mother in your old age—your saviour? Or was I the punching bag, so weak and gullible that you could push me around at will?

Do you realize how girls like me understand manly love? We accept disrespect and dismissal like a baby learns to crawl and walk.

It started at work. I accepted bad behaviour and could never complain about harassment, as I felt that perhaps I had brought this upon myself. I couldn't ask for a salary raise. I just did things in autopilot mode.

I often felt like a plastic flower in a vase, which had no fragrance. And the petals did not shrivel, but stayed in their place, lifeless and, over time, discarded.

Love,

Manu

14 February 2023

Delhi

Dear Baba,

Do you think a woman needs a heartbreak insurance fund?

To help her cope when the man who promised her the moon, the sun, loyalty and respect, suddenly forgot all that he had said to woo her?

To women—
who have loved and lost,
felt broken
and over time
courageously looked back and
marvelled at the evolution of
another human being
who was a partner in this life journey.

May you pick yourself up
knowing that if you had it in you
to give so much of
yourself to another being.
You can do it for yourself too.
Just change the goalpost.

You may feel weary.
The burden of the unfairness can be excruciating
it might feel like the walls are closing in
or
the ocean bed is swallowing you into its dark depths

You might wish you could wash down the pills
the doctor prescribed for a good night's sleep
all of them
all at once
but
know that the heart that's broken
is the strongest of them all.

Sit down
put your hands on your lap
count your fingers twice over
feel the strength of you and your soul
after that
ask for no explanations
as most answers would be lies
it might be
as black as the soot in chimneys left unused for years.

Instead
think of ways to replenish the self.
In some cases
you may be alone.
In some with the warmth of friends
or
it might be a generous fund!
And in some
there may not be even an apology.
But I promise you
it will be freedom
sweeter than wine
cleaner than the soft morning sunshine.

This fund
may save you from the rain
stitch your torn umbrella's gaping holes.
So hold that close
and slowly walk away.
But don't forget to shamelessly get
the heartbreak fund
If you can.

Love,
Manu

17 February 2023

Bina Ramani's guest house,
Lado Sarai, Delhi

Dear Baba,

I am angry and resent the fact that you have pushed me to a corner where I find myself constantly questioning my feelings and the validity of my thoughts. I gave you unflinching support and devotion; you were always so unsupportive and critical.

My pillars have all let me down; none of you could see how much I hurt. To add to the misery was the separation that caused so much anxiety.

You wronged me.

The time has come for me to resurrect myself. I have to fathom who I am. Who is Mohua?

I often wonder why I feel so guilty for asking for a fund for my well-being. It's as if I am not supposed to ever think of myself. Why are we taught that we must look after our family selflessly, without expecting anything in return? How unfair is that?

Eventually, we are all individuals with a separate heart, a separate brain and viewpoints. At one level, society asks us to be individualistic; in the same breath, we are urged to forgo ourselves.

Let me tell you about what I witnessed during my walk in Delhi's Lodhi Gardens one afternoon. I saw a squirrel, a parrot, a bowl of water and some grains around it. The squirrel was holding on to the grains. The parrot was pecking at them, too, and then their eyes met. The parrot lunged at the squirrel with its sharp beak. The squirrel scurried up a tree and did not return. The parrot had won. It strutted around and pecked on the grains. Basking in the sun, occasionally fluttering its green wings, the bird's red beak picked each grain, one by one.

I feel one with the squirrel.

I know it's my share that I am asking for as a fund. Yet, I am frightened of the red, sharpened beak of conditioning that will bruise me if I ask for the money that belonged to my husband and me. I always felt that I didn't deserve it, so I was consumed by guilt.

You have been willing to share a part of your earnings with others, but not with me. Why did you never ask me if I needed any money? Instead, you only wanted money from me.

I draw a blank when I hear about people loving their children, of couples in love. My pessimistic mind would like to believe that most human beings are unable to find a common ground. They marry thinking a union would be a wonderful path to sunset. It isn't.

I saw you and Ma together in dark clouds, in tandem outwardly, but so different. But then so many couples follow different paths to converge at one singular path later in their lives. Many women are embarrassed to even think that their paths won't ever meet. They live forever unfulfilled. I think if they comprehend the lives they have led, they will see fragmented pieces of themselves when they look in the mirror. So many won't know how to deal with unfairness, infidelity, anger and disrespect; most will think all this is their own fault. 'Why can't I keep my man happy?' they will ask themselves. 'Is it because I am too fat, or too thin, or have small breasts, or small hips, or am I just not beautiful or sexy enough?'

Truly, does a woman's happiness count?

Did it matter to you that Ma was alone mostly through her married life? You were both so young. You were so beautiful together, and so distant. I couldn't understand how you ever closed the chasm.

You were always critical of her. I never looked into her eyes to see how she felt. It's only now that I see those eyes welling up. But not a drop falls. The tears stay like a swollen sea that churns inside her but doesn't flood the land ahead. She is like that now—like dry land.

Don't you think a woman should be insured as a housewife, as someone who manages a home with no security? She gets a certain amount of money to run the show. But what happens if the man gets over her pregnant body or tires of her fragrance? He moves on, and deep inside, he is aware that what he loses is nothing compared to what a woman has to face. A woman loses her place, sometimes her home and, in terrible situations, her children. Shouldn't she be compensated for the years, for investing in the relationship? The government must have a system in place for stay-at-home mothers. The penalty she pays with her life must be compensated.

I am so glad Ma was a working woman. Did her career bother you? I remember Ma said it did, but I don't recall you asking her to quit her work. So I guess you both were progressive in your own ways.

Love,
Manu

18 February 2023

Bench overlooking a tomb,
Lodhi Gardens, Delhi

Dear Baba,

I wonder what you think about women—whether it's Manu, your daughter, or Ma, your wife, or Thamma, your own mother. Do women need to find the 'real' themselves or carry on with the role assigned to them as daughter, wife, mother? What do you think?

I think of all those women out there who have woken up from abusive relationships, parental pressures, of not being allowed to nurture their passion—even if it's something as mundane as arranging books on a bookshelf, I salute them. I fear I have not been very smart, and have been fooled by wolves in sheep's clothing. As little girls from a convent, Little Red Riding Hood was a favourite character of ours. These fairy tales became a part of our inner psyche as the years rolled by. We were learning not to question the gender play in these tales—that a handsome prince saves Cinderella from her cruel stepsisters and Snow White from her cruel stepmother. You nurture the fact that someone has to save you, to help you fulfil your dreams.

Today, after having been fooled for years, I am looking for answers. I am troubled by this intense lack of respect for all that I sacrificed and this disdain for daring to question the status quo. I do feel broken on many days because this feeling of self-doubt hasn't been purged yet, it keeps coming back, asking questions about why we, as women, nurture and consider the home that we create as a sanctuary. There are times when I resent…when it feels like I am stuck in a time warp.

Like most men, my husband got the better part of the deal in our marriage. He could nurture his career, his passion, and his idea of the self. Also, as he grew socially and financially, there was travel across the world. I was stuck being a caregiver.

I was always there, alone, when anyone in the family had to be admitted into the Intensive Care Unit, as you frequently were, or when my child had his final exams or fever. It was never anyone else's responsibility; the unspoken rule was that I had to do it all. When I was bedridden, I endured it alone. I had to be this powerful Devi, but when it came to running the home, I had to be strong, yet demure.

I must say I was happy to be seen as a dependable person. I didn't know then that there was no one I could depend on. Ma said I had to be grateful for the good life I had. I didn't understand why I couldn't tell her that I was tired of all this. I keep wondering why you didn't stand by me when I was bleeding. Why was I supposed to understand that it made you uncomfortable? I was supposed to learn to accept that—but I was young, naïve, and not made of iron. I was hurting, too.

I understand now that in most homes, it is someone's monetary position that gives them respect, and the entitlement to not shoulder familial responsibilities. I, having shouldered many such responsibilities, realized that

I had no financial power and that I had become unhireable.

I made a pact with myself and decided to stall my dreams of becoming the next big communication specialist as I moved cities and became the reluctant homemaker.

I learnt to push those dreams away when I saw the happy Sunday faces of comfort I had created. I suppressed the self, but found joy in you all, my family.

But now, after all the pain I have endured, I'd be a fool to trust any of you again. We women accept that we need to remain behind the scenes even when we know we are as capable as our spouse. But we ensure that we don't hurt our men's fragile egos.

Women often complain that their partners seldom have a conversation with them about issues that bother them. So the women give up trying. Like the others, I was expected to bury my sorrows.

Do you remember Pamela, my friend from Delhi? After ages, she called today. She has decided to separate from her husband. I could relate so much to all that she said. Most women sail in the same boat. They just don't realize it.

Pamela said she felt sorry to see what her husband was turning into. She said, 'He is inauthentic and not true to the spirit of who I am. I feel like a fake in the company that comes along with his social rise. My soul is getting corroded and I have no control over it.' I felt helpless listening to the despondency in her voice.

'He used sex with young women to prove his power. His expensive clothes covered the internal childhood bruises he had, and the weekend alcohol was to numb his pain.'

Pamela asked about you and Ma. I told her you were

no more. The words again felt unreal to my own ears.

Pamela said she wanted to leave Delhi and restart her life. She was sobbing when she said, 'I have to be a fool again to trust him and I will also lose respect for myself if I continue after all this water that has flown but isn't under the bridge yet.'

I understood Pamela's grief wasn't about her husband's infidelity as much as it was about the entitlement he felt as a male. She said she would see someone to hurt him back. I couldn't tell Pamela that she needed to let him go.

I gently told her to take up work. 'Yes, I want to, but I am insecure,' she replied. 'The real me wants to live with my family, love them, cook, listen to songs, maybe work in a mountain café with my husband and write a book of the years of solitude in a home as a housewife.'

'Ditto,' I said.

'Why would a woman want a man who had slept with so many women,' I asked Pamela. 'Can he just come back and say "I love you"? If this isn't abuse, what is?' She kept quiet, and then said, 'He says he only loves me.'

She said he called her beautiful. They made a good couple with the right clothes, the right car and the right job. But when they partied together, she would remain in the shadows, be as unseen, as demanded by her husband. But Pamela was beautiful and she couldn't be ignored.

'I know vodka will help me sail through this pretence. Yes, I have mastered this art of looking happy with unshed tears inside. He fills my glass every time it's empty, compliments me in public, but doesn't desire me when we are alone.'

Pamela said that she used to watch him from a distance—the lies, the inauthentic person he was becoming. 'Who would believe me? He was a good student, a good boss, a good friend, and an understanding colleague. Yet it was so easy for him to not be good to me at home, where no one was watching him. Everything was like a practised speech,' she said, 'like a show where the best liar won.'

I laughed and told her to make him the protagonist in her book. I realized she couldn't smile at that. 'Bored housewives like you are finding fault forever,' he told her.

I sobbed with Pamela. I knew Pamela felt very alone. She needed to brave the storm.

I could see Shawn, Pam's husband. I wondered whether when he was alone and took off the Hugo Boss, the Montblanc and the Rado, did the real person emerge?

I thought of Pamela that night as the pillows mopped up the leftover mascara. I realized I too had felt let down like Pam. To compose myself, I would look at the moon-faced baby sleeping next to me. In a jiffy, the world seemed better.

Just like Pam I too have learnt to forget my woes and hold my baby like a bobbing oar in the choppy seas of treason. If this isn't bravery, tell me what is.

I wrote for Pam and other women:

Someday I shall find myself
in the arms of someone
who will love me right.
Like he has never loved anyone better.

Someday that love will
maybe show me the stardust,
the blue clouds in the fading horizon
like a painting.

Someday I will be brave enough
to march into the unknown
where the cup is full of love
and it brims over with sunshine
soon...

Someday all of us women
will find ourselves anew there
in a utopia
that is fair and equal.

Love,
Manu

2 September 2022

Bengaluru

Dear Baba,

You were extraordinarily intelligent. You had great disdain for anything flippant. I used to be in awe of this unbelievable ability of yours to remember dates of history. How could you remember them all?

And how did the store of knowledge just vanish? When dementia started creeping in, you shouted out for me in the hospital. You said you wouldn't leave till your daughter came to take you back. The nurses had to hold you down. Your cheeks were wet with tears. You turned to me and said they had found radium in your blood. They were selling your blood, you said, and the money from it should be given to Neel. I could not, or rather did not, want to believe the disintegration of that sharp mind that I had known.

Negotiate the price, you said over and over again. I nodded as I watched you wither away.

But what torments me still is that even in your delirium you wanted the money to be given to Neel and not to me. Did you miss a son so much? Were you filled with sadness because I was born with a vagina? Did you see a son in your grandson? But I guess the best part of being your daughter was that you loved my son.

You had a mean side, deep inside you, that made it seem like you hated me. Why?

Neel had the good fortune to meet you when you were

in your prime and get enveloped in grandparental love. I feel I can let go of my pain, just for that.

It is difficult for children to explain what it means when they are not cocooned by their parents. Betrayal by one's parents stays ensconced in the ribcage.

Love,
Manu

5 September 2022

Bengaluru

Dear Baba,

I felt so abandoned when the autoimmune disease took over my body. None of you believed me. Instead, you said my pain was imaginary. With so much disbelief around me, I, too, started to think that I was imagining my distress.

I learnt to hide the feeling of abandonment during my extreme pain, till it came tumbling out like a skeleton from a beautiful gift box that had been tied up with a silk ribbon. I felt like that.

We don't discuss emotional abandonment; we are encouraged not to talk about it. I dread to think of those married women who feel abandoned in illness and in the misery of their married existence. They are not expected to talk about it—even with their parents or friends. But parents' responsibilities don't end with rearing a daughter, and then getting her married.

I faced such harshness when I rebelled and married into a family that wasn't open to outsiders. I was made to feel unwanted. But I am stoic, so I stood my ground, rising above those demeaning, unspoken gestures, words and behaviour. But what happens to those who can't stand up? Who do the helpless ones turn to? Do they just accept their fate and stay chained in humiliation and solitude?

As a young girl, I was encouraged to overlook toxicity. I was taught to be silent. I stayed silent—till resentment turned into rage, overwhelming my spirit and body.

The disease showed up in spasms of pain, which lasted for a few seconds, and then later for days on end. It first affected me physically and then mentally. Slowly, my body started to give up and the mind was no longer able to fight the disease. And you and Ma were not there for me.

Was I that unlovable?

Love,
Manu

31 December 2022

Bengaluru

Dear Baba,

This year will remain etched in my heart. This year, I stopped being a daughter to a father. I could never understand how girls were raised in fatherless homes. How could they live without knowing the association with the first man in their lives?

I must admit that at one level, I was relieved to cede the caregiving duties I had unknowingly signed up for. The responsibility was gruelling, emotionally unbearable most days and exhausting. I have come to understand that I have actually been a parent to both of you from the start. It's just that I didn't sign up for therapy earlier to understand the psychological impact of all that I went through—your reactions towards me, the meanness. I wonder what healthy parental love feels like.

I cannot comprehend how much I wanted to please everyone around me. I tried so hard. Today, I have finally found closure—I shut out people who don't accept me, and embrace the ones who do.

I wasn't hassled about the 'why' and the 'how'—and the 'why me' again. I suppose I was fated to be a parent to you both—each of you so needy, trying to overcome your emptiness.

Where did the emptiness come from? I would like to believe it was this constant move from city to city that caused this emptiness, taking such a toll on your mental health. It's not easy to find the mundane and the marvellous in every new city. Moving is like surgically cutting away the life where you found your little corner of sunlight; it's like the little crevice from your broken windowsill where the moonlight entered. Imagine the house you know so well. That little dark corner where the sunrays catch the cobwebs. You hold up your fingers in that, watch the graininess of your being, like sand. The sand that you fill in your palm, and then slowly let go. That moment between holding and falling marks the senselessness of leaving a place you have known for the unknown.

I am sure you were riddled with these questions. That little Shillong boy, searching for a life away from the poverty of thought in the narrow walls of familiarity. Those thin walls through which you could hear the neighbour cough. In that claustrophobia, maybe you found a home. What made you both so unwelcoming to people around you? You buried yourself in books. You made your regular doctor visits your outing. I would go with you. Post that, we ate lunch or had coffee. I do miss those days.

I remember the day I took you to the hospital for surgery to reduce your vertigo. I remember Asif, my friend and colleague, helping you out of your clothes. I neatly folded them and kept them on the bedside. Your white cotton vest, pants, belt, side strap bag, and a small pouch that you kept strapped across your hip. They took you to the operation theatre.

I sat listlessly, watching your things. I feel choked when I think of that now. I wish I had held on to the fragrance of your old, decaying body. The wrinkled skin. The face, those eyes. All of you.

What I remember is that I wanted to cheer you up after the surgery, and took you to a restaurant that served Kolkata Chinese. You dropped the food. You apologized to the waiter and tried to clean up the mess. I sat there, watching the mess, saddened that you were not in control.

We three were a mess together, weren't we? Like the fallen noodles, strewn around that table. I was consumed by guilt for taking you to a restaurant. Something took me back to Shillong. The time I was learning to eat with my fingers. You said, 'Don't eat like a hen. Eat without pecking on your food.' That statement stayed. I got neater.

It must be so hard to have one child. You hate being dependent but you have no choice. You both were fortunate that you could come to Bengaluru. Imagine parents who are left alone to look after each other. Most are bitter with life—yet in that bitterness, they learn to bond. In hospitals, I saw elderly couples who had no one else to accompany them. I was glad l was there for you.

I remember your apology to me, too. One day, as you sat in the wheelchair, you looked at me and said, 'Sorry!' I wasn't sure what to say. I felt a lump in my throat and said, 'Don't worry! This is the least I can do.'

Ma feels so lost now. She no longer wears her saris but wears an ugly nightie she wouldn't have touched a few years ago. She is waiting to leave me.

She sits with her hands cupping her face. Is she thinking about what is to become of her? Her eyes seared into mine as if asking me to forgive her.

I look at her with love, distaste and sadness and wonder how a daughter deals with parental betrayal. You both continually betrayed me. It was unfortunate that I couldn't articulate my thoughts when you were alive. But you anyway didn't want to listen.

I often think of the time when I offered to donate my kidney to you, and you rejected the thought. You were self-righteous in many ways. And sentimental—longing to return to a home that was lost in debris and debt, like an entire lot of Bengalis who'd fled Bangladesh—something that you could never return to.

I wonder what happens to them? Are their children studying abroad? Are the parents alone? In an old-age home? Who will they call out to when in pain?

Maybe deep down you wanted the freedom to relive your life once again. But how does a dying man take his daughter's kidney? You couldn't, so you just looked away.

Ma is helpless without you. Not that the love between you two was visible, but you had one another. I have no one. No one to tell me, 'Hey! I got you.' So I have not much regard for your love, if at all there was any. Your conversations about me were all about my wrongdoings. This may have given you the energy to communicate with one another.

How do parents bond over meaningless rants about their own children? I don't understand that. I would like to believe that I am fiercely protective of my child.

My child is far away from me. I wish that he stays safe and protected. I often miss his baby days, with his head on my shoulder. He is the only one who seems to understand the complexity of my life.

Where will I go, what will happen to me? These are questions that I ask myself. Some days I feel tormented, being able to find the river that ran its course so smoothly over the rocks. Those little flowers looking up at the sky. I am frolicking, my feet submerged in the water. Its cool calmness engulfs me as the winter sun warms my cold heart. It's torn and needs fixing.

Love,
Manu

REDISCOVERING MYSELF

1 January 2023

Bengaluru

Dear Baba,

In the New Year, I resolve to do many things. First, I must come to terms with pent-up anger, the feeling of being wronged. I have decided that I will no longer wait to be seen, heard or understood.

But I do remain convinced that you both were unable to find any fault in my husband. Even if you did, you chose to stay with what would bring peace, overlooking my heart. This made me bleed.

I feel insecure and frightened about such a large transition. There is less communication now between us. Unfortunately, we need time before we can become civil. But staying in touch with Chini helps me feel less alone in this city.

The truth is, my ego won't allow me to admit that those lame, abbreviated text messages—a good morning, and a goodnight—though done for the sake of duty, did help me feel less alone in a city that I feel trapped in. But then I think most human beings are trapped—in a web of lies. We tell ourselves that tomorrow would be a better day. But it's actually all the same. We just get used to the pain and the disappointment, I guess.

Love,

Manu

28 February 2023

Bengaluru

Dear Baba,

Sometimes I wonder if I will feel loved again. When will that 'someone' come to put a hand on my shoulder? When will that 'someone' walk hand in hand with me, into the morning light?

I wait for that 'someone' to fiercely stand up—for it's scary to face the world without a filter of speech, vision, opinion, and even your own reflection. Filters help you protect yourself from the judgements of patriarchy, the narrow walls of social norms steeped in dos and don'ts for women.

I watch myself closely: over the years, lines have appeared on my face and the lines of propriety blur my soul and spirit.

After all this turmoil of trying to understand who I really am, I still haven't reached that level of freedom and awareness where I don't have to apologize for who I am. I am sure so many of us stay silent when we wish to say, 'Sorry, but no sorry.'

It is mostly the real me talking to the real you—with the scars and lines of defiance.

To me, filters are a sham.

Filters are nice only in photographs. In your persona, they are most unattractive.

Love,

Manu

15 November 2022

Bengaluru

Dear Baba,

At times I wonder what shaped your response to me. On one side there was this deep, unarticulated love; on the other, acute criticism of whatever I did. Why?

I have no answers.

Maybe the seed of diffidence was sown early on, when your Borda, elder brother, who was a revolutionary and, in an uprising, went missing, never to be found again.

You narrated to me so many times how Thamma, your Ma, lost her mind when she lost her eldest son. As your condition worsened, you wanted to go to the river in Bangladesh where you believed your brother's body was thrown after he was killed. Tears rolled down your grey sunken cheeks, and we sat helplessly watching you.

I couldn't hug you or hold you as I had never experienced your hug. You were awkward about any physical form of affection. You pushed me away or moved away as if you'd been bitten by a bug.

Maybe you didn't receive any form of physical affection from your Ma and Baba? After all, you were one among 11 children.

I remember Thamma so vividly. Her big, fair face, her extremely dry skin, her white sari, and how she ate from a special stone plate. She would say her prayers, and then we—her grandchildren—would sit across her as she gave us dollops of rice mixed with mashed potatoes and ghee. Its taste still lingers.

She moved to Benares (now Varanasi), wishing to live a life without attachments. She wanted a pious end. But she came back—to your favourite elder sister's home in Shillong. She was happier with her daughters than with her sons' wives. I was too young to understand those gender equations.

As I look back, I wonder why you longed to reconnect with your dead sisters and brothers. What made you want to go back to Bangladesh and look for long-lost cousins who'd stayed back after the partition? You longed to see the temple in the place where you grew up, and the river that had turned red with the blood of all those boys who'd fought the war. In that bloody mess was your brother's blood.

As I write, I see your ashes in the terracotta urn, bobbing, floating in the Kaveri River in Karnataka, as it winds its way to your family. You may have already met them in the ocean of the afterlife.

But you left me here, waiting for you to show your love.

Love,
Manu

3 March 2023

Bengaluru

Dear Baba,

Becoming a housewife was not a decision I took knowingly.

The truth is most women don't know what to expect after marriage. The ones who appear normal on the exterior don't let it out if they have regrets. Over time, their years of regret harden like the curd they set for the family. Did you ever closely observe the delicate setting of curd? It looks beautiful and white. But if you cut a slice from the set curd, it starts to spill and crumble. Some women are like that—they know their regret can come pouring out, like spilled curd, leaving a sour taste behind. So they learn to restrain themselves and resist the urge to speak up, lest things sour.

I still can't forget the day I quit work and decided to be a stay-at-home mom. At first, it was Neel's shiny baby face. It felt awesome to be there for him. There was trepidation, for I didn't know what to expect. The first day was fun. I did what I had yearned for. I woke up fresh. I dressed Neel up for school and off we went to the bus stop. It felt so fulfilling to wave bye-bye to him as he boarded his school bus.

My childhood wasn't like that. Ma had a job. So I felt that the decision to quit was right. As the days passed, I made a routine out of Neel's life—going to school and coming back home. In between were the other pursuits of self-care and an odd coffee with a friend. Most were housewives who were on a diet or trying hard to ensure the child attended maths tutorials. They spoke a language I didn't understand, but I nodded and smiled. As time passed, I didn't quite realize when and how time had flown. It was now over a decade. Then, suddenly, I was rudely awakened by this sweet lullaby.

I thought of going back to work several times while Neel was growing up. Those pangs came when I had to ask for money or when I thought of the future, of what was to become of me.

As a family, we all had different paths. We gathered on Sundays to talk. The set routine started Monday onwards. I buried the thought about going back to work as soon as it began to rob me of my peace. The truth is mothers barely think of their own future. Mothers believe that they must be selfless. So they train their minds not to waver. They look after the home and get attached to broken vessels. I, for one, can't imagine my kitchen without that kadai with a broken handle. So we think of our children's educational future and the husband's job. We remain obsessed with the present. Nothing matters beyond the visible levels of marital success. Our internal issues, our aspirations can wait.

We think, why worry about what's ahead? We learn to hide the jumbo under the carpet. And is that when we become redundant? What happens to a housewife when gadgets take over her manual labour? Or when marketing companies make food designed to individual needs?

But it was lovely to be there for Neel. To pick him up from school. Drop him to the bus stop and wave him goodbye. In planning his tiffin…his classes, football and tuitions. It was all very purposeful. But I had no idea what to expect when he went to study abroad.

I'm trying to find my feet, Baba.

It's sweet to deal with maids, plumbers, electricians, vets and paediatricians, but when no one needs you any more, the resultant loneliness is a tough pill to digest.

Okay, let me stop here today. I have a playlist on Spotify to listen to.

Will resume talking to you tomorrow. I have no clue if you are listening with intent or your usual disdain at my 'feminist' rant.

Love,
Manu

20 December 2022

Bengaluru

Dear Baba,

I don't know where I belong. Shillong? Or Delhi? Or do I belong in Bengaluru?

Unlike you, I don't know if I will ever belong anywhere. We talk about being uprooted from a place of familiarity. But what is familiar? Shillong, with its constant bullying on the roads, in school, in the neighbourhood? Delhi does seem familiar when it comes to language and places. There is a greatness about big cities—you can get lost, or find yourself in the fabric of a city that doesn't really belong to anyone. No one cares that I am a Bengali, which is such a change from Shillong, where you felt you had to cower because of your identity. So yes, Delhi seems a little like home. The memories attached to our government accommodation in Delhi evoke the feeling of community living. We knew what was cooking in the neighbours' homes. But the city was rough too—unsafe for a woman. Can I settle in Delhi ever again? I don't know.

You were so sure of Kolkata, of finding joy in the city. You always said you felt connected to Bengal. Not West Bengal, but Bengal. It gave you a sense of home. You were lucky. At least you knew and could recognize what was home to you—the feelings of rest and peace. Peace seems to play hide-and-seek with me on most days.

If I didn't speak to you both once a day, I used to feel

like a ship sailing into the dark sea, towards a destination that had no end. I felt tormented not knowing who to talk to in a language close to my heart. If I missed calling you, I used to be engulfed by grief—how could I forget to check on you both? I did that almost every day, sometimes twice a day. You both were so dependent on me. This is the price we pay when we choose nuclear families; the price is paid as we grow older.

In my head, I always told myself that this is what children were meant to do for ageing parents. Check on them, involve them in their lives, speak with them. But you took me for granted. Sometimes you forgot to disconnect the phone after we'd said bye, and then I could hear you both criticizing me. Was it because I was a daughter? Was it because you both had made no friends, in the 20-odd years in Bengaluru? Did you feel terribly isolated in this city you could not call your own?

I do understand that moving from a place of familiarity isn't ever easy. One has to learn to restart life all over again. You did so too. You gave up friends, support structures, family and relationships that came naturally to you. Suddenly you had to learn a new language. You moved from Shillong to Delhi when you quit your well-paying government job to join an engineering consultancy in Delhi, to earn more money. But you were fortunate to have been in Shillong when Thamma passed away. Ma was not so lucky. Dida passed away in the morning. They found her stiff in the evening. Her daughter-in-law was in school, teaching kids. Ma felt guilty, devastated, and didn't know how to say sorry to her mother. For leaving her in a place where she never really felt at home.

I often think of Dida. Married too young to a widowed man. Dadu was married to Dida's elder sister, who died at childbirth. Dida was the Mashi, the maternal aunt, to their children. So it was natural that most felt she would be the perfect woman to look after her elder sister's children, and she was married off to Dadu. But in spite of a life of duty, Dida was unwanted after Dadu died. I can't begin to understand the trauma and grief she felt after losing her husband and son and becoming an unwelcome guest in her own home. What goes through the minds of such women at the fag-end of their lives when they don't have a place called home?

Which place did she yearn for? Faridpur, now in Bangladesh? Did she yearn for Kolkata? She prayed to Krishna, chanting that the day had finally come to an end, and she needed to cross over to the other side of the river. Which river? The Padma there, or the Ganga here?

Just like I see Dida, carrying her grandchildren's school bags in the relentless heat of Delhi, bringing them back from school, I can see you too, Baba.

In different places. In Bengaluru. At my home. In Kolkata after your heart surgery. In Shillong. I see you again and again, walking down the streets in your chequered blazer, a sweater, your brown corduroy pants, muffler and a beret. That walk was sure-footed and happier than the last walk to the hospital.

You sent me photos when you went to visit our home. The home Ma shifted to after moving from the joint family system. It was brave of Ma to break away from the large home where your parents lived with you and your then-unmarried siblings. She looked out for a rented home to shift to.

She wanted to find a new place that would be close to her office and my school. With the help of a shopkeeper in Police Bazar, who knew the family well, she found a house with a large compound. It brought her the independence and peace she sought.

It reminds me of Satyajit Ray's *Ghare Baire*, in which the protagonist changes as she breaks the rule of stepping out of the cordoned area for women. Ma stepped out of the joint family home with her belongings and set up a home for her nuclear family.

The house had five families with separate spaces within a compound, somewhat like a gated community housing one finds in cities nowadays. Each home was occupied by Bengalis from East Bengal. There was no unfamiliarity in the little oasis there. The house has all my memories of Shillong. I know that they are yours, too.

Ma was surrounded by friendly Bengali neighbours. But you found it empty, cordoned off, an unclaimed property. You sounded so sad. I heard you sigh. In resignation and an emptiness that echoed in the sky on a moonlit night.

The moon reminds me of our Shillong home. The moonlit skies. The lull afternoons, a song playing on the radio across the hills. The bamboo trees swayed as the hills stood stoic under the azure skies. You and I missed that sky; actually, all three of us did.

It was oceanic blue, with fluffy clouds. I remember the rain-drenched roads, the blue hydrangeas and the trees that made a sound like a whistle, or a kiss, or maybe a long-lost tune.

You understood that we could no longer return to that peace. You had travelled ahead in time and distance.

I am unsure whether you could even relate to the people you left behind. But you were sure that the common language of Bengali would bind you to the place you had left, that which you searched for in the dry, arid plains of Delhi and the broken roads of Bengaluru.

I remember that day you were so angry with your failing kidney that you left my home to walk back to yours. You were weak but certain that you did not want to be in your daughter's home.

There were days when I was rude—you made things so difficult for me. You stopped giving me that stare you used to subject me to because by then you knew you were dependent on me. This further angered you. Your dependence and your decision to move in with me were a bitter pill for you to digest.

If Ma had this ailment, it would have been so much more difficult for her. I wouldn't have taken it as seriously as I took your disease. Because she is a woman, my Ma must bear more than what anyone else can handle. The expectations we have from our mothers...

We expect the mother to love her children unconditionally but we are more adjusting with the father. Why is that?

Why don't four walls make a home?

I find myself going back to Shillong, your friendship with Afzal, the owner of the Karuz furniture and photography shop and a theatre actor. You would visit him, with me in tow. We sat together as you both spoke. You carried me back home. I must have been three or four years old. But I remember those days. The eucalyptus trees and the smell of the pine cones scattered on the roads. The sloping roofs, the rainbows, the bakeries and the biting cold.

I guess your heart lies in Shillong. As does mine.

Love,
Manu

8 March 2023

Bengaluru

Dear Baba,

Ma is unable to do anything. She can't come to terms with life.

Why is it that we believe we will remain young forever? Most of us live thinking the end is distant. So we quarrel, we don't say sorry and we live with resentment.

I try very hard to remember the good times with you. I have to think hard. The bad times were so tough that the good seemed like a sliver of light in dark, foreboding skies.

How would life be for me when I age? Will my house help be there at the last hour, giving me a sip of water, or putting a 'tulsi' leaf over my eyes?

At home, I have Suleman Hussain Khan, our driver, but more a home manager. He is a Bengali Muslim from Agartala. It helps that he is Bengali. We speak the same language. A Bodo Christian girl, Zarina, motherless, with an uncaring father, does the housework. She is laid-back but trustworthy and rises to the occasion when needed. There is our Nepali Brahmin cook, Mahesh Bhatt. He wears a sacred thread. He has mastered Bengali dishes—Bengal's typical *niramish* (vegetarian) and *amish* (non-vegetarian) food. He knows how some dishes need to be tempered with only garlic, and how you don't add garlic or onion in those vegetarian dishes. They all support me unflinchingly—and that is my blessing.

So I wondered who would do the rituals for me.

Maybe I will be in senior living and will pass away peacefully. Like the leaves Neel and I collected during our walks in New York's Central Park. The beautiful strewn leaves had soundlessly fallen off the trees. I do pray that my end is silent, too. I should go like those leaves.

Leaves that are used in a bonfire, or an inspiration for an artist.

Love,
Manu

9 March 2023

Bengaluru

Dear Baba,

How long does one take to overcome deep grief?

How does one process grief? Do we ever process it? Or does grief lie around like crystals found on the riverbed, embedded in moss and the gurgling water? Over time, the moss covers the grief and nothing can be seen. But the niggling pain remains and never leaves. Or does the moss get washed away in the river, and grief flows into eternity?

Ma carries her grief with her. She is unable to bear the loss of her partner, friend and companion—you. I watch her health deteriorate. She crouches in pain.

She now weighs 45 kilograms. She is skeletal; the bones stick out of her body. Everyone is full of well-meaning suggestions for her. All she does is nod at the advice doled out. And then she sheds it like old leaves from a tree.

I keep thinking about what would be peaceful for her now—death or living on.

In her heart, she wants this suffering to end. But I am selfish—I want her by my side. I want that look from her when I dress up to go out. She likes it that I look like you. She was young when she had me. So naturally, we both fought, made up and kept our secrets forever.

As I watch Ma, I realize women become vulnerable when they lose a partner, but men become more fragile as they age. They lose their sense of life when they lose their wives.

Women sometimes recover from the loss; men seldom do.

How do I, as a spectator, process this heart-wrenching end of a life, and soothe Ma's anguished heart?

As for me, I held you both as the most solid and permanent people in my life. But I am growing to learn every day that life is transitional. We come alone and leave alone.

Ma didn't want to eat today. Then, out of the blue, she asked for some potato chips. 'Okay,' I said to her, but before that, she must have her barley and milk.

Even Neel wasn't so demanding.

Love,
Manu

10 March 2023

Bengaluru

Dear Baba,

Ma hasn't been well at all. She eats very little and throws up whatever she does eat. She asks me to bring her *rasgullas*, and some days she wants *payesh* or chips.

I am exhausted. I was your golden child, but my lustre is wearing off.

I'm still trying.

Love,
Manu

11 March 2023

Bengaluru

Dear Baba,

Admitted Ma to a hospital. Hussain stayed the night with Ma. I chose a single room for her as I find it very difficult to work and be a caretaker too—and share space with others. I deserve comfort as the sole caregiver.

As I paid the initial deposit sum, I wondered about the innumerable people who come to Bengaluru from different parts of India for treatment. How do they manage the costs? I worry about them.

Today I used the GPay app to pay the initial amount. I requested Chini to put the money into the card so that I could manage the expenses. I am grateful to be able to do this for you both, but I end up thanking him for the money. I keep wondering why housewives have no say in the wealth the family creates. Why do I hesitate so much? I still have to delve into this sense of worthlessness.

Ma is in the room, but frightened of everything. She doesn't have your support and her dependence on me is sometimes clingy. I know she hates this feeling of helplessness.

I need to tap into my inner source—into the divine—to understand why I am here to do seva for you both.

If my Shiva—the divine—stays with me, I will be able to be there for her. You had made me promise that I would not put her in an old-age home. I would never abandon you. So why did you need to say this to me? Is old age so full of insecurity and trauma that you can't trust your own? Or has displacement broken you both so much that you just can't get out of that feeling of despair anymore?

I often think about how life would have been if I were your son. How would I have navigated between my household, you two and my wife, who may not have had the same sense of love and duty towards her in-laws? Perhaps all three of you would have adjusted. Like two spoilt children, you wanted most of your wishes to be fulfilled by me—yet deep in your heart, you wanted a son.

Anyway, this is what you got. A daughter who bore a son.

Love,
Manu

3 April 2023

Bengaluru

Dear Baba,

I had an amazing interview today with K.K. Raina and Ila Arun. It was surreal. They are coming to Bengaluru with their play. They spoke very passionately about a play on postpartum depression. This issue has not yet been addressed by society. A woman who wants to express her depression post childbirth is not encouraged to speak up. And she fears being judged and looked upon as an incompetent mother. Becoming a mother along with raising a child is a project in a woman's life. Motherhood is an exalted status, but no one is willing to talk about the pain that motherhood faces.

K.K. Raina spoke about how he left Kashmir for Delhi and joined the National School of Drama, or NSD, as it is known, on a scholarship. He did films with Mrinal Sen, Govind Nihalani, Shyam Benegal and many others. As we spoke, he broke down while talking about his father who didn't speak with him for six months when he joined NSD. Then, one day, the actor went to perform in Jammu. The local papers carried articles about him; many people asked for his autograph. That time, he invited his parents to his theatre performances. As he spoke about the incident, he became emotional and started to cry.

He is 70 years old now, and can't forget the sadness of being spurned by his father, or what must have been the immense joy of being finally accepted by him.

Parents play such a pivotal role in a child's healthy upbringing. On the other hand, a parent can scar a child forever with casual remarks, and an inability to accept the child's decisions about the future. Many parents make their child their parent, though most do it unknowingly. They became parents by chance, too, for it was just the natural course to be followed after marriage.

Things are changing now, with women choosing not to have children or worried about their biological clock ticking away. Women are more informed today and have, if not full, at least partial autonomy over their bodies. And I think that itself is a start.

As I spoke to K.K. Raina, I travelled back in time. I remember when Neel got constipated after he started solid foods. You came with me to Manipal Hospital to get him checked. As we finished the consultation and walked out of the room, we passed a mirror. I saw our reflection. You were there with Neel in your arms. And I was there, with my hair all dishevelled, my blue kameez unbuttoned, my nursing brassiere showing. On my kameez was a trail of milk. I had put on so much weight! I couldn't recognize myself. I stopped for a second and felt tears roll down my cheeks. I was managing my new-found role of motherhood alone. But I had to be competent, able and responsible.

I held a cry in my stifling heart and felt suffocated. The past seemed like it had melted away into a place unknown. The jagged icicles that remained poked into my heart, reminding me of who I had been just a year earlier.

Had I been the one who walked down power corridors as a Public Relations (PR) professional, who won all business deals, and spoke with ease to the chief executive officers (CEOs) of companies and media houses? Who then was looking back at me? I had no clue.

I looked at Neel and saw what a beautiful baby he was. In the first two months, he kept me up most nights. Then my life fell into a pattern.

I shudder to think of Thamma who had had 11 children. You were one of them. Neglected, unloved and later displaced. Perhaps your anger and resentment were valid.

But you both were great grandparents to my Neel. I will be eternally grateful for the love and joy that Neel received from you both.

Neel and I smile at the memories of those days when you argued with him about his various ideologies.

As I cleaned your side table today, I found a small red book with Mao's famous quotes. I let the book lie there like the way you would have wanted it—so that you could reach out at night and read it when no one was watching. The tattered leather wallet with your State Bank of India (SBI) debit card and a Spencers discount card were there. I held them and said thank you.

You both helped me navigate the birth of Neel in the hostility I faced as an outsider in my extended family. I was distraught but your constant reassurance—and the fact that you came to Bengaluru for me—kept me together on those days when even the sunset made me cry.

Love,
Manu

1 May 2023

Bengaluru

Dear Baba,

I have learnt to make my own payments. I check my bank accounts. The only thing still left to conquer is the inability to learn to walk away when I feel slighted.

My work is appreciated. I regret that you didn't think much of my intellect, but the world at large has been moved by my podcasts and writings. So I guess it's all good in the end.

Just today a Hindi publisher offered to publish the translation of my debut collection of short stories. They are giving me a small advance against royalty. I'm thrilled. If you were around, I would take you both for a lavish meal or a trip somewhere close by.

I do miss you and your joy of travelling to new places.

I feel quite tired today. Will speak soon.

Love,
Manu

24 February 2023

Delhi

Dear Baba,

Yesterday was very special. I was invited for dinner at a friend's home. As I entered, I saw there were other guests. Near the entrance was Ustad Amjad Ali Khan Saab, the God of Sarod. For a few seconds, I lost my sense of time and place. His face glowed as if the moon had decided to shine only on him for the night. I found my way to sit next to Ustad ji's wife, Subhalakshmi. She looked as regal as him. She was loving, kind and unpretentious. She is my Loreto Convent classmate's Pishi. As I got my glass of wine, we started to talk about Shillong. We spoke in broken Assamese and Bengali. After some time, Ustad ji came and joined us and we discussed religion, music and life the entire evening.

Ustad ji said, 'Music is transparent, you can't fake a good tune and sound. We learn rhythm when we are born. It is the heartbeat that is the first sound we hear. It changes tempo based on our emotion.' As he spoke about Ustad Bismillah Khan ji and his guru, he gently touched his ear.

I thanked Ma and you for going beyond your means and admitting me to Loreto Convent in Shillong. The school did teach me how to hold a conversation in a place such as my friend's last night.

You told me how you met Allaudin Khan, father of Annapurna Devi and Ali Akbar Khan, and father-in-law of

Ravi Shankar, in Benares, when we were on a project there. You were both in a fish shop buying fish. As you spoke with the shopkeeper, Baba—as Khan Saab was called—asked you if you were a Bengali. You told him about your roots in Bangladesh, and he invited you to his home for a fish meal.

I remember the way your face lit up when you spoke about all the great artists, writers and revolutionaries who had made an impact on your young mind.

Love,
Manu

3 February 2023

In bed, Bengaluru, 5 a.m.

Dear Baba,

I have been feeling hot flashes as if I am near an exhaust vent that is blowing hot wind into my body. I want the fan switched on as well as the air conditioning. I ask those around me if they are feeling hot, too. Most say they are fine. I think I may be having a cardiac arrest. But then the flashes pass on like Shillong's pregnant clouds. Those clouds that promised rain and then ditched the flowers waiting for showers.

I steady myself, hide my embarrassment and realize it is menopause knocking at my body. The hormones have decided to do a tango without practising the steps. I suddenly experience a sharp pain in my breasts, which then slowly reduces. The pain comes and goes in waves. At times it is sharp, like the way my breasts hurt when I missed feeding Neel. I felt thorns on my lactating breasts; they seemed so unfamiliar. My breasts had a different character then. But once again they are tender and they hurt. The difference is that I won't lactate any more. It's the same cycle from the start to the end. Like life and death. That, and the end of fertility, reminds me of the amazing magic of a woman's womb and its end.

The heatwave makes my face go red. I feel the heat coming out of my ears. I am told that this is the end of feeling sexy or desirable. And to an extent it's true. I feel being celibate is the most beautiful way forward. I love my sleep more than ever and the idea of losing that seems like hara-kiri. Celibacy is like protecting the self from the sexual violence endured by people who are not in love, and who have no sexual chemistry. They continue with the act of sex without listening to their body, heart or mind.

Also, how does one verbalize the term menopause? Most of us have learnt to bury the end of womanhood, which is naturally associated with the end of fertility. So we learn to cower and hide in shame once we stop menstruating. It is spoken among friends in whispers and it must remain hush-hush.

Unknowingly, we have imbibed that our worth comes to an end if we can't procreate. As women, we have learnt that we can't publicly speak up about menopause without running the risk of being viewed as someone whose shelf life has come to an end. Unlike older men, who apparently age like wine, women age like milk. It makes me want to scream out and yell that this is unfair, so horribly skewed and insensitive.

None of us can foresee the end. I try to focus on my spiritual journey. I understand that into dust we all will go. It takes me back, again and again, to the time when your entire body was in a little urn of ashes, and reminds me of the person you were. Those hands, eyes, the shining face—all gone in a jiffy as the crematorium workers pushed your dead body into the fire. I didn't comprehend that this was the end.

I remember you saying, 'I am like a drop of rainwater on a lotus leaf—shaky, constantly trying to balance myself.

Soon, I will vanish into the muddy water, and flow away.'

I don't understand endings well. So I don't quite comprehend this end of a part of my body. It feels like freedom from recurring mouth ulcers, the sharp pain in my calves and then the uterus walls shedding again for four days. Will I miss this? What I may miss is the inability to feel a full woman again. But I am a woman. Just not a menstruating one.

In this ageist society, no one is willingly going to speak up about the freedom that comes with menopause. The joy of not worrying about the unannounced blood spattering out of the uterus. We tell our friends, almost apologetically, that we don't bleed any more. We are apprehensive of the reactions, scared that we will be called a hag, an oldie, all dried up, a sweet old lady, and so on. The start of fertility is a long-drawn battle with our bodies. Some of us go under the knife to remove the uterus; I, like some others, undergo the pain of IV injections to stop the unending bleeding.

I felt so humiliated when I had to spread my legs for the gynaecologist, as she checked my vagina and said, 'Watch out for the bleeding. If it continues, consider surgery.' I was angry about the abortions I had and how I had messed with my hormones. But at that time, I felt I wasn't ready to have another child. I knew I could raise one well, anything beyond that would not be within my bandwidth. This angered many.

With pre-menopausal life, it was a new journey. The bleeding would continue for 10 or 11 days. The bed sheets would be soaking in fresh blood in the middle of the night as I felt the warmth seep. I felt angry. I wanted to apologize to my body and seek its forgiveness. But it was oblivious to my scream.

Then, one day, a friend suggested I meet an Ayurvedic doctor. I was unsure that I'd ever heal, but miracles do happen. I met Dr Azeem at his clinic—and found my saviour. He was gentle, smiling and understood my thoughts. He asked me to take some pills. I did so, and in three months, my periods had regularized. Dr Azeem was my healer and friend, and it was always such a pleasure to visit him. He spoke about his family and enquired about mine. The conversations were always gentle.

Finally, the angry womanhood settled into a rhythm. It's been many months since I bled unexpectedly. I still carry my sanitary napkins in every travel kit, but they come back untouched.

Back in Shillong, Ma used to hide the sanitary napkins under her sari pallu. Bleeding was a matter of shame, even a sin. I was not supposed to tell anyone that I was bleeding. I obeyed, like always. I remember the cloth pieces that Ma had made for me during the start of my periods so that no plastic touched my skin.

I remember the start of my periods in Shillong. You were sitting and reading; Ma was at work. I told you there was blood on my thighs. You said, 'Go wash up, maybe you've hurt yourself.' When Ma returned from work, I was squatting on the bathroom floor, with a line of dark brown blood flowing out like a stream.

Ma took me aside, cleaned me up and explained that I had become a big girl now and I must not run around too much for the next few days. 'Do not tell anyone about this,' she said. I felt as though I'd been cursed.

Over time, the cloth that Ma cut up as sanitary napkins changed to pretty packets, the elastic ones to the stick-ons, and then the tampon. And finally, this journey is ending for me.

I do hope more women open up and share their experiences about menopause so that we form a circle of sisterhood to help each other in this lonesome and challenging phase of our lives.

No, I am not a hag, and definitely not curdled milk. I am divine, at one with my intellect and spirit. My ovaries are like an ocean bed, holding the little flowers, seashells, the oyster with a pearl of wisdom nestled in its crevice.

My love for you is infinite and I miss you so much.

Love,
Manu

26 December 2022

Dear Baba,

Today was the 100th episode of my podcast, *The Mohua Show*. I never thought I'd be an entrepreneur after being at home for 13 years. But there is something to be said about that old adage—where there is a will, there is a way.

I recall those conversations I had with my friends about wanting to write and start a podcast. No one took me seriously; some may have laughed at me. I didn't feel bad, because we are tutored to not feel. I think this is the way most women do it. When she stays at home for too long and doesn't earn, she is not taken seriously by the world at large. She accepts it and, over time, forgets who she was and blends in with the ones who don't question the purpose of their lives.

This vacuum is like a well, and she has to have immense courage to delve into her inner reserves to be able to reboot again. This isn't easy at all. A stay-at-home woman is unceremoniously called a housewife—but there are no words such as an outsidewife or househusband. A housewife finds herself at a loss over time. I too was the same. I was rudderless—till I had to face an empty nest and the empty cupboard space. I didn't know what to do to feel worthwhile again. My value in my own eyes had shrunk. I couldn't find the answers or the path back to my own self.

I do speak on behalf of so many women who, like me,

give up work, give up their lives to run a home. Over time, the house becomes their identity, their place of pride and their idea of self-value. And sometimes these things fall apart. When that happens, most women feel derailed and devastated.

But I carried on, disregarding harsh criticisms, and even your look of disdain. I held on to my mission of creating a space for the unheard to be heard.

I still recall the time I interned as a journalist for *The Sun* magazine. The resident editor had little faith in me. I liked to dress up, and I think if women are fashionable, they are considered flippant. So I was mostly not taken seriously. I remember how he smirked and said, 'If you want to be a journalist, get me a one-on-one interview with Khushwant Singh.' As an intern, I felt intimidated. But I was also stubborn. I looked him square in the eye and said, 'Okay, I will get it.'

I had no idea how I'd do that, but I was not going to give up. I asked around and then found my way into Khushwant Singh's Sujan Singh Park residence one day. The interview went smoothly and he said, 'Come back if you need any clarification or another interview.' Then he winked and said, 'You know my reputation with good-looking women.' I smiled half scared, half assured. I thanked him and got my advance copy of *Sex, Scotch and Scholarship,* his then still-to-be published book, signed.

The article did get published, and the editor looked somewhat stunned. I proved him wrong; and again I proved the conception wrong about age, time, place and conditioning that women were bracketed into. Rebooting wasn't easy but it wasn't impossible.

From *The Sun* magazine, I moved to *The Observer*. I had my media card. I felt most powerful with the word 'media' embossed in red on the card. But I left journalism to join public relations. I did very well in that and learnt how to market myself and other brands.

But it wasn't enough. Ma wanted me to settle down, and I, too, felt that it was not enough to just have a good career. One had to marry, like all my friends had done. But I had moved away from your middle-class Bengali lifestyle. I decided I would not marry a Bengali, and went on to choose a man from Coorg. I'd had enough of Delhi, too. The city seemed to restrict me; I wanted to spread my wings.

I confided in you about wanting to marry Chini. We arranged to meet over lunch at a restaurant in Nehru Place. Chini was a bit nervous, but I was sure you wouldn't dislike him. I had the freedom to think beyond the box, unlike many others.

'Why do you want to marry my daughter? She doesn't even know how to cook,' you said to Chini. Chini replied he would find a cook.

That night at home, you, Ma and I talked and laughed. You joked that Chini had no idea what he was doing. I was glad all was well. But Ma said the next day, 'We won't stop you from marrying anyone, but a Bengali boy would be better for you, Manu.' I laughed and said, 'I don't want to deal with a balding and paunchy chap.' But Ma was serious. She said, 'If you plant a big banyan tree in a pot, the roots won't grow and the foundation will remain weak. We raised you as a Bengali. Maybe you don't realize it now.

But to not be able to speak and express in your mother tongue will feel soulless over the years.'

I wasn't one to be deterred. I was sure I wanted to marry and leave Delhi, and start life anew. Also, I expressed myself in English. I had no clue how I would hold on to the nuances of my mother tongue over the years.

As a privileged member of an upper caste and a large community, I must admit I didn't understand the predicaments of a smaller community. The marriage took place. But I was too young to comprehend that acceptance wouldn't come easy.

Do all women and men who marry out of their community or religion have to face criticism, denial and discrimination? How does one understand all this at a young age, when we are in love with the idea of a loving relationship, whereas the truth is that the relationship is driven by practicality? It was hard on me. Once again, years after Shillong, I was made to feel like an outsider.

With marriage, we moved cities. The cities were smaller, as were the opportunities.

It wasn't easy being the national head of the PR division of a large advertising agency, where working mothers' woes were hardly given any consideration then, back in 2013. The culture was male-dominated and there were many instances of women being sexually harassed. I brushed those off as the downside of the advertising world. Or I thought I'd brought it upon myself.

The autoimmune disease took over my body and my work. As I gave up this senior position and the growth that would come with it, my world shrank further. I tried part-time work so that I could be back before Neel returned from school. But my identity was crumbling at breakneck speed. So was my body. I popped painkillers and visited doctors during the day when Neel was at school.

When I left all work—big or small, even the little consulting jobs—I felt I was finally learning to overlook my ambitions and become a good mother. I wanted to be there for my child, unlike Ma.

It felt good when I started meeting other mothers and Neel's teachers and having play dates fixed at my home, where I could keep an eye on him. I knew that finally, I could attend cultural programmes with my child. I again found myself getting deep into raising my child and also enabling an environment for my husband to thrive in. I was happy being the giver and enabler, yet always in the background. I smiled sheepishly when people said, 'Behind every successful man is a woman.' What they didn't say was—'Behind every successful man is a disillusioned, gaslit woman who doesn't comprehend what she is giving up!'

Things changed as we both grew older. He became more successful and I became more hesitant. It was one thing to enjoy your child's grades and guitar lessons; it was another to find yourself asking for money, month after month.

I didn't realize I was losing myself. People say that the bored housewife doesn't know what to do. I knew what I couldn't do—I couldn't sell jewellery or clothes. I was bad at negotiating money. I only had mastery over words, my ability to listen and put them on paper.

But I knew that I disappointed you all as I fluttered my wings to fly over the horizon. I wanted to find new places among the clouds, among stars and the bright sun. I had shaken off the chains of restraint to find myself anew.

Love,
Manu

3 May 2023

Bengaluru

Dear Baba,

It has been a tiring day. Going through the drafts of your own work isn't easy. As I sit down to drink my black coffee, I wonder what happens to old housewives. How do they navigate life, if the spouse decides to leave or maybe dies before her?

Imagine a situation when a woman, who has never ever worked her entire life, wakes up one day from her slumber and realizes that she had signed up for loans on behalf of her dead husband and she barely has any savings. How will she pay back the loans? Does the family system, the law or the state protect her? Do activists do anything for women at home? Or are they merely discarded like peels?

Becoming a housewife means you are agreeing to do unpaid labour, remaining insecure and constantly seeking approval.

Who in their right mind would ever agree to this arrangement? But sadly, women do. A young girl is brainwashed to happily give herself up to have a family—that may one day fail her.

There are also many men who think they are the breadwinners, so their wives shouldn't earn. They believe the male ego gets bruised if the woman in any way has the capacity to be independent of him and not depend on him for her needs. Many women are gaslighted into believing that this is his love for her. He wants to be the provider and she needs to be the nurturer. This way, the control dynamics stay in place forever.

You travelled so much. You won't remember many of our neighbours. But I recall an aunty from our neighbourhood. She was very pretty. Her husband didn't keep well. One winter evening, as I was returning from work, I saw her walking with a young man. She could be recognized from a distance. Her body was slender and her long hair swayed on her hips. Her son perhaps was 23 or 24 years old back then. She wasn't with her son.

She was with another man, young enough to be her son. They walked hand in hand, into the darker alleys of the colony where the street lights were dim. I was right behind them. I could see the bangles on her wrists.

Why would Aunty be out with this young stranger, I wondered. I was too young to comprehend that she may have needed love, and the desire to be heard—elements that were not there in her marriage or in her life as a housewife. She could meet no one but the colony aunties, who were mostly judgemental.

As she walked ahead, I thought of the house she ran. During Sunday winter afternoons, Uncle used to sit in the warm sunshine as she served him parathas on a steel plate. Her *ghunghat** stayed in place. Her beautiful hands with those glass bangles served him his tea and breakfast. He would eat without looking up.

---

*It is a headscarf, generally *aanchal or pallu*, the loose end of a sari that is pulled over the head and/or face.

I used to watch them together. They were together—but not really in sync with each other. I also remember Aunty used to keep money in her blouse, inside her brassiere. I used to laugh about that. So one day she explained to me that this was her own money to buy the nail polish and the bindis she wanted. For that, she wasn't answerable to anyone. She used to collect the change when she got a good bargain while buying vegetables.

That day, as Aunty walked leisurely, I slowed my pace so that she wouldn't spot me and get embarrassed. She didn't turn back. She continued walking. She was laughing, and his body brushed against hers. She looked animated and happy.

I understand today that all she wanted was to be desired. She may have found someone who loved her back. And it wasn't Uncle.

Maybe this young man liked her hands. Under the dim street light, the two looked surreal. He was definitely going to leave her heartbroken as he was younger. She would get back to making yummy parathas in which her love wouldn't be there. It would have the stench of duty and rejection that never reached anyone's nostrils. She wouldn't express herself and say that she needed to feel better as a person, as a woman. But as a housewife, she had no choice.

Love,
Manu

5 May 2023

Bengaluru

Dear Baba,

Just how threatened can the world feel by an empowered woman? The developments in Iran seem unreal. Education is banned for women in Afghanistan—and girls wanting to study in Iran are being killed.

I am distraught by the news of schoolgirls being poisoned in Iran; this blatant effort at gender subjugation in the city of Qom. The Iranian Deputy Health Minister, Younes Panahi, said the young girls had apparently been poisoned because they wanted to study. And education was barred for them.

It leaves me in shock. How can anyone rationalize this abhorrent act? The Taliban has constantly condemned the Western way of life. They don't want their culture to be influenced by the *haram** of the West. So in that ideology and condemnation, women become the torchbearers of societal morality.

I was hoping to talk about this with someone I met today. I don't have too many people with whom I can discuss political changes in India and across the world. You were so communicative in matters of politics, but you are

*Or the impermissible, which is defined as an action that one firmly seeks to abstain from and whose perpetrator is entitled to censure and punishment as per the Islamic tradition.

not there. As I write, I can see your face contort in disgust at this oppression of Afghan and Iranian women.

The woman I met today is rather young, perhaps in her 20s. She said she was looking for work. She seemed earnest but was lost in her own thoughts as I rambled on about Iran. Then, out of the blue, she blurted out that her parents wouldn't have allowed her to marry a Muslim man. She said she had had a crush on a Muslim boy, but she didn't take it further. She is an upper-caste Hindu woman and believes that life is easier for her in India. She said she would have been subjugated in his conservative home, been covered from head to toe like his sisters.

'Perhaps not,' I said. 'He might just be the opposite of what you think,' I pointed out. But she was sure he wouldn't go against his family. He was the eldest and would need to continue with the legacy of carrying on the family tradition. He would be with her only if she converted to Islam. I realized I was getting annoyed with her vehemence. Conditionings are for real. Love is there, but only when no one is inconvenienced. Love is mostly about what society expects of a relationship.

I dropped the subject. The heat was getting to me in the café. I could see the sunlight streaming in from the dirty exhaust above. The blades had darkened with grease, but a ray of light fell on the table. I held my glass of water against the light. As I twirled it around, the water moved—and I was transported to someplace else. I thought of the girls who were dying breathless in Iran. I looked into the water and felt a pair of eyes behind a veil look back at me. I put the glass down and pushed it aside. I couldn't look at it. I felt my stomach churn, imagining the plight of the girls, poisoned by their very own.

The woman opposite me was speaking about how disconnected we were from the real struggles of minorities. She was sure we would never understand the perils of being a minority in India, or the world. How hate towards Muslims, in general, had become a tool and a poison that is being fed to the Muslim commoners, who are clinging on to tradition and archaic ways in fear of losing their identity.

The poisoning, perhaps, is being rationalized as a commitment towards the community and the upkeep of the faith. So are parents not to be trusted anymore? How does the very womb that protects you also poison you?

I looked away, but the young woman carried on. She had a nasal tone. Killing girls because they wanted education was the lowest anyone could ever reach, she said. It was shameful and blatant to keep a girl chained so that she could not leave her country or her home. She was glad she didn't pursue her relationship with the Muslim man, she said, though she admitted she thought of him now and then.

I told her that the poisonings flouted the tenets of humanity, not just religion.

'But injustice happens all around us,' I said. I asked her to take a look at the café we were sitting in. We could easily see the cages, those cages in which little birds are kept. Those cages that have golden chains and a small bowl of water so that the pet birds can quench their thirst.

'You can spot subjugation and oppression in this very café,' I said. We looked at the women there, most of them in semi-expensive brands. But they looked vacant and stared into their coffee mugs lifelessly. I laughed. We are like the Iranian women. The only difference is that we are educated and free, yet still chained to customs prescribed by our families. By now, I had her interest piqued.

I told her we too learn to poison our own minds and hearts. We rein in the poison, keep it covered so that we don't question the status quo.

It is not really our fault, though. This poisoning starts early on at home, where our mothers and fathers are biased. But why do people cling to traditions that hold no value? Also, why are women always the target?

There are no answers to these questions.

Just as there is no one reasoning as to why human beings turn to ash or dust.

How can a small earthen pot hold your remains? How can I deny a relationship that courses through my blood? How do small acts of children reflect the genetic traits of parents? How are we connected to our children and our parents? How do parents sleep after poisoning their children, whose only fault is defiance?

Men in homes where women are subjugated are blinded by a mindset that seeks to hold on to a system. They may feel threatened in a society that requires them to think differently or critically.

But how does one justify this? Murdering your daughter whose only wish is to study?

I feel exhausted.

More in the next letter.

Love,
Manu

28 February 2023

Khan Market, Delhi

Dear Baba,

It's a warm day in Delhi. Summer is around the corner. The remnants of the adjoining desert sand are all around, making the leaves brown and sinewy. The winds from Rajasthan's Aravalli mountains have swept through the city. It is arid and dry.

Delhi is only beautiful in parts. Poverty stalks large parts of the city, with migrants trying to find their space in this metropolis. Yet, Delhi, with all its squalor and aggression, makes you sigh as you suddenly find yourself staring ahead at the Qutub Minar in the midst of maddening traffic.

I went to Khan Market today. I took the lane at the back, with all those cafés and stores. I stood near Faqir Chand Bookstore and saw a board that said: 'Estd. 1951'. This was there way before I was born. I imagined you as a young boy in Delhi coming to this bookshop.

The shop had books all around, placed in a haphazard manner. I wondered how anyone could find what they wanted there. A few customers browsed inside. It was like the old times when people had only one form of entertainment—and that was to read.

It reminded me of our trip to Kolkata, and visiting Boi Mela. It was so amazing to be with you at the book fair; you ran around like a little boy in a candy shop. You went into the Bangladesh pavilion to look for new authors. As the world waits for upcoming trends in clothing, accessories and lifestyle, you wait for new books. You stood there, bag on your chest, the beret on your head, staring at the rows of books. I soaked in the sight of my learned Baba.

Then there was the Chapala Book Stall in Shillong—the only bookshop that sold schoolbooks. I especially remember the Bengali exercise books and the brown paper you both bought to cover my books with. The word for it in Bengali is *molat*. Some words and things stay with you but will soon become extinct. Those newspaper cones that contained *jhal muri*—puffed rice mixed with mustard oil, peanuts, chillies and pieces of coconut—will soon be gone. Physical books may disappear one day, too.

Do you remember the lane to the Chapala Book Stall? And Arun Restaurant, which sold a thali with dried fish and rice? I remember the places as vividly as I remember you reading and poring over your books. How you loved to chat about books, especially literature and history!

You have a knack for appearing suddenly in front of me in some form, or perhaps the universe points me to a memory tied to you. As I stare at the books in the Khan Market store, I find a book reaching out to me. It is Irving Stone's *Lust for Life*—a book that you loved about an artist you admired.

Everyone loves Van Gogh. It's easy to love the man and his art. You had prints of his work, and the desire to see his art was one of your unmet dreams. You spoke so much about the artist's longing to be loved and understood.

Did you feel one with him?

I know you too had a lust for life. What is a lust for

life? Yours must have been to go back to Shillong, be with your family and maybe become young again. Walk those lanes of fading memories, mistakes that you would treat differently or choices that, in hindsight, you may or may not opt for.

I end here today. The vision of you reading and standing in the Kolkata book stalls makes me miss you so much. But if there is anything called an afterlife, we may meet again. But this time, perhaps, with a little less lust for life—and some more kindness.

Love,
Manu

1 March 2023

Delhi

Dear Baba,

I think women get destroyed when they stay home as housewives. There is a motherhood and a housewife penalty that a woman must give with her life if she chooses to do this. It is not easy to get out of the tight grip of this web. Many women lament the lost years, and that they ended up not earning. In most cases, women lose their self-respect and are broken when their marriages unravel. I had no option but to reboot. This old life of the same uninspiring shit was getting to me. I had to pretend I was enjoying the company of people who were never close to me. So why waste time, I told myself.

But rebooting isn't easy, especially for women who are stay-at-home mothers and housewives. Their world is narrow; the playing field is only the drawing room, the kitchen, the bedroom and the balcony. One can live forever in a cocoon in that environment. But what happens when marriages fall apart? Where do the women go, those who have never navigated the real world outside?

I know women who don't know the way back home. They led a steady life—met the regular set of women in the building's recreational space, where they kept an eye on their child who was playing with other children. They conversed with some housekeepers who had come there to watch over their employers' children. Sometimes, they met the grandparents of a child. I have done that too. My favourite time was when I took Neel out in his pram. We took rounds around the building every evening.

My world was limited. I was engrossed in raising my child and enabling my husband to grow in his career. He grew, and I was left alone in a corner after Neel left. I found it difficult to express myself, to say that I wanted to work, reinvent myself and become more than someone's wife or mother.

It felt bad—and I was made to feel small—about voicing my own needs. 'You must look beyond yourself' was the constant message I received from everyone, including you, Baba.

But my day-to-day activities—being drawn into the entangled mess of the house help—became frighteningly regressive for me. Initially, I felt good being needed and purposeful when my staff sought me out for advice and help. But when Neel left India for his studies, I realized I needed more for myself, from myself. That vacuum left by Neel forced me to think afresh.

Why doesn't society support women who want to start anew? Why is it that everything becomes so unbearably difficult for women if they want a new life? Society seems to sneer at us, saying, 'What audacity to want more than what you are being given!'

As I sit today in Delhi, away from the sound of home—Ma hobbling around and waiting for me to make her laugh—I feel glad to be away, but miss my home too. I have been eating alone and sleeping alone in a new environment. I do worry about being alone.

The only thing that helps is work. It makes me feel

less alone and maybe writing will become my companion as I grow weary and tired. But the thought of becoming feeble scares me. I wish to die in my sleep. Easy and quick.

You and Ma are fortunate to have had me look into every little detail of your lives. But this may not be my fate. I may just find myself alone in a home for the elderly.

I went to meet Uncle. You remember Mr Biswas, the lawyer from Delhi High Court who lived in the next lane in R.K. Puram? He was very fond of me. He spoke about literature and law with equal ease. His daughter and I were friends. She messaged me on Instagram when she saw my Delhi visit stories. There was no way I could not visit them. So we fixed a Sunday when everyone would be at home. Uncle and Aunty have aged. Aunty's mother, who is a widow, was there. She had shut herself in the room that belonged to Aunty's daughter. The daughter was angry that her room had been taken away; Aunty was annoyed about having to look after her mother. She was complaining about space. I was alarmed but stayed cool.

Deep in my heart, I keep thinking what becomes of women who are widows and have only daughters married into patriarchy? Where do such women go? Do they die alone? Also, what happens to men who lose their wives, and have only daughters and no sons? Where do they find their anchor?

Recently, a business tycoon found love at 91 years of age. But not everyone is so lucky.

More again.

Love,
Manu

30 November 2022

Bengaluru

Dear Baba,

Finding love is the hardest thing ever. Some say it is all about how lucky one is but, according to me, it could also be a blessing from a source that remains elusive to those who are needy like me.

Love is so difficult to find, but when it comes, it doesn't last. It dies the death of a hungry pauper. Love comes, but in such short spurts that it leaves one wanting more. Isn't there anything called lasting love? It seems like a fairy tale—a great story but not lived by anyone, only read. And perhaps found in dogs and their masters.

Most of us crave romantic love, the basis of which is so transient. It is in most part sexual and some part emotional. Most people mistake sexual chemistry for love. We are frightened to answer what happens to couples when they don't share that physical chemistry any longer. Do they lose out on their understanding of love? Then, do they desire another? Or do they just stay mum?

Today was quite special. I was sitting in an Airbnb owned by Bina Ramani when she walked in. She took over the room with her infectious aura. She sat like a queen and gave me a birthday gift of a set of beautiful beads she had strung together. She spoke about her life as a refugee from Karachi and being a Sindhi. She said for Sindhis, there was no state in India they could call their own. She spoke about her ex-husband. And how today, at nearly 80 years of age, she wants to rest and only think of creative matters. When she goes out for a walk, the trees and branches all around her speak to her in languages that she hears. When she tries to sleep, night urges her to expand her creative journey further. I feel the same when I watch sunlight fall on trees and leaves and enter the corners of the rooms.

It was amazing listening to her. 'Any sort of human suffering,' she said, 'was the first step towards enlightenment and growth.' When we suffer, we say, why me? But once people overcome this self-doubt, they are glad to have withstood the storm, however shaken up they were then.

My personal catharsis began when I first decided to write a book and start my podcast. It was the start of a journey of freedom. But I know that not everyone is fortunate enough to find themselves. Most women give up searching for their selves. It is so difficult to force ourselves out of our shells. The shell is cosy and warm. It gets washed away by the force of the sea. It has no personal need to find new shores. Women who are like the shell are fortunate. The problem is with the ones who are looking for the sea and not thinking of the depth before they dive into it headfirst. The seawater enters our eyes and mouth, making it impossible to breathe at times. The process of finding the clearer sea of reason involves a tough swim, often going against the current.

I was so scared when I started searching for work. At one level, I didn't know what I could contribute to the field and, at another level, I knew that if I put my mind to it, I could. But very few were willing to put their faith in me.

I remember once, over a phone call, you teasingly called me the CEO when I had lost my work. You called me the CEO of my home. I felt bad. Those days I didn't know who I really was. I think I took too long to figure out my groove.

For days I thought I was the home in charge, like a glorified maid. Or did I even really mean anything to anyone? Was I capable of thinking anymore?

The answers are fuzzy and I feel sad you didn't explain to me the reason behind the deliberate hurt you caused.

Is this what is love? Where you take each other for granted? Is it like the oyster on the seabed, elusive and unreachable?

As I write I can see you and Ma sitting on the seashore, watching the waves go up and down. Is this what you call love?

More later.

Love,
Manu

11 May 2023

Bengaluru

Dear Baba,

The process of reinvention means the end of the old, decaying parts of the self that no longer serve a purpose. Past equations change. Some friends who were never actually your friends come out of an unopened cabinet like worms. It isn't easy to handle such a change, but it's not impossible either. Some days are frightening; some are buoyant like a river pregnant with hope.

In Delhi, it's been great meeting new people and sharing a part of the new me. Today, I met someone over coffee and she called me a non-conformist. I was unsure how I did not conform. While sitting in my car, stuck in the traffic of Delhi, I think any woman who restarts her career in her late 40s must have a lot of nerve. Reinvention means different things to different people. For some, it may mean being isolated in the treacherous journey to find oneself. For others, isolation can be maddening. So some may find it easier to handle their new selves by spending time with close friends and family—with people who don't want you looking or acting in a certain way. The lucky ones spend time with families where they don't need to pretend.

Many rebooters learn to hear themselves and find their voices for the first time. But the path to reach that space, where you learn to listen to your inner voice, is a difficult one.

Love,
Manu

13 May 2023

Bengaluru

Dear Baba,

You were driven by wanderlust. I inherited that. I too love to travel the way you did. You always spoke about how one mustn't become a frog in a well, frogs that think the well is the world and nothing exists outside that. They cannot see sunlight in its full glory.

I especially remember our train journeys together. You, Ma and I had gone together to Kolkata. We stayed near Gariahat and you took me to eat biryani at Aminia. You explained the significance of the potato in the flavoured rice to me. I still remember your smiling face as you watched me dig into the food. The small details never leave the heart.

Then there was our trip to Darjeeling. Like all Bengali families, we went to the hill station. You wanted to watch the sunrise over the Kanchenjunga. We were huddled in a jeep with two other travellers, waiting for the golden rays to bathe the snowy caps of the mountain. Ma wanted to use the toilet and missed the sunrise. We had our camera and an Eagle flask filled with tea. The memories are so fresh—the road uphill and the little glasshouse coffee shop that overlooked the mountains ahead.

There was no conflict, only a lot of sunshine and happiness. We holidayed in Puri; we went to the beach, collected seashells, went to the Jagannath temple. Ma got Odisha's silver filigree hairpins for her long hair.

We also travelled with Neel to Puducherry and Kerala. There was such bonhomie when we dined out every evening. You sat with your beer, and I with my vodka. Ma disapproved of us enjoying a drink. Neel laughed with you and Ma. Those were golden moments and my best ever.

It was stupendous to see you work beyond your retirement years. You wanted to continue working. You loved being productive, travelling and exploring new places.

I remember our trip to London—visiting the Tate Modern, taking photos at Buckingham Palace and eating in restaurants. You spent a night in Neel's room. What an amazing bond you had with your grandchild. I think he fulfilled the part that you found missing in me.

On the last day, as we were leaving London, you tipped the doorman and chuckled. 'It is a dream come true to tip a colonizer as an Indian,' you said in Bangla—and I laughed. You were the quintessential, witty Bengali. You had such a charming and deep bond with your external world.

So many small and big things pop up in my mind. I went by air for the first time from Assam to Delhi. At the airport, we met a group of actors and Ma urged me to go and say hello to them. I remember walking up to the late actors A.K. Hangal and Nadira, and how they laughed with me. Ma mistook a door for the washroom, and I was embarrassed. All those memories stay sharply etched in my heart. You could afford those flight tickets because you had made a large amount of money on a project. I remember the gold hoops you got me for Pujo. I remember the toffees given to me by the crew, the perfumed tissue packet that I kept for so long, as a cherished memory of the flight experience. I was in class three. India is a sum total of so many cultures, as I learnt during our trips to Benares. We sat on the boat and watched Manikarnika Ghat, which Hindus believe is a holy place for cremating the dead.

I remember the dead bodies being burnt, and the temples. The hotel window that looked into the Darjeeling hills. The seashells from Puri. The fragrance of the bookshops in College Street in Kolkata. Your final rites in Karnataka.

We can never ever be sure where we end and where we start. It has been a journey for you, for sure.

Love,
Manu

16 May 2023

Delhi

Dear Baba,

I was very troubled last evening. Every time I am anxious, I tend to overeat, and then feel guilty about it.

I met two friends over lunch yesterday. I offered to pay, but my credit card didn't work because of insufficient funds. I felt ashamed. I saw the look in one friend's eyes; the other kept saying it was okay, she would pay. The bill was for ₹2,000. I was so embarrassed that tears came to my eyes.

How do housewives live their entire lives asking for money? When they do get money, it's as if a favour is being done to them. The problem is this gaslighting, the desire to keep women subjugated and in control. Most of us find no fault with this. Society frowns at attempts to quantify housework. Women have been fed for generations that housework must be done out of love, duty and affection. I think we need to question this belief now.

With a heavy heart, I finished lunch and went back to my Airbnb.

As the sun was setting, I saw birds returning to their nests. The summer sky was a pretty pink mixed with blue; cirrus clouds made a sweeping brush over that artistic canvas. I felt calm watching the birds. At least they don't have gender roles assigned to them, I thought.

I felt nostalgic about Delhi, though there is nothing of

our Delhi life there any more. I wanted to visit the temple Ma took me to—the Dakshin Delhi Kalibari in R.K. Puram. The temple is built along the lines of the Dakshineswar Kali Temple in Kolkata, with a red dome-like structure. It was like a slice of Bengal in the middle of Delhi.

The *arati*[*] was being conducted. The Goddess was dark and feisty and had the most beautiful Bengali gold jewel-crafted crown on her flowing hair. It was the most exquisite workmanship I had seen in a long time. She looked ethereal. I could see Ma, her younger self, running down for the Pujo bhog.

I sat and watched the devout pray. The purohit started the puja. The ambience changed. There was the sound of the *dhak*[†] all around me. The Goddess' face had been lit up with the lighting of diyas.

I missed the days when we were together.

I did a video call with Ma and she looked teary-eyed as she watched the arati. I took my phone around to show her the place. 'Are the rooms still there?' she asked.

I said, 'Yes, they are there.' Every Kali Bari has rooms where middle-class Bengali visitors can stay. They take the rooms on rent, and the kitchens serve Bengali food.

I recalled the time when you both had stayed there. I had no claims over our family earnings, and couldn't afford

---

[*]Arati is a ritual employed in worship in which light from a flame is waved to venerate deities in Hinduism. It also refers to the songs sung in praise of the deity.

[†]It is a huge membranophone instrument, and the drum beats are an integral part of Durga Puja. The enchanting beats are enough to conjure up the sights and smells of Pujo.

a better place for you. It took me years to fight for a right over the money earned.

Ma and I spoke and I could hear her anguish, which seared into my heart. I know she was missing you. I too was missing us. I decided to leave the temple. The flowers were in full bloom. On one bench, a girl was sitting, continuously scrolling through her phone while her parents were close by.

I wanted to tell her, 'Go sit with them.' These days won't last and the holidays will end but you will endure years of inner turmoil if you lose the familiar place you find yourself in today.

Love,
Manu

26 February 2023

Delhi

Dear Baba,

I went to the ANHAD office and met Shabnam Hashmi today. They completed 20 years, fighting for minority rights and gender equality. I took part in the celebrations and the singing. There were many left-leaning people—comrades, as they are called. They sang songs, peppered with slogans of 'Inquilab'.

My toe hurts. I was trying to get into my car, and my foot got stuck in a rope, which almost pulled out my big toenail. It started bleeding, and I felt alone. Very alone.

The driver was a kind man. He got me a Band-Aid and put it around my toe. I felt a lump in my throat. Thank God for people and their kindness. I am feeling very low today. I wish our home in Delhi was still there. I would return home to Ma's cooking and, like before, after my evening bath, eat rice and fish and sleep peacefully.

But where did my home go? Where did I go? Why do women have to leave their cities to join their husbands? Why is it that only women have to do this adjusting?

But I am at ANHAD. The celebrations—and the cries of Inquilab—remind me how you would repeat the word 'Inquilab' when you were losing your mind to dementia. Was it delirium or did you still seek a revolution? I have no answers. All I remember is the angry you, frustrated when you lost yourself, inch by inch.

ANHAD has beautiful flowers in their garden. Shabnam and her husband Gauhar are amazingly well-mannered, good people. I feel fortunate to have met them. It's like an old world of good manners and etiquette.

I know you would've enjoyed meeting them thoroughly if you were around.

I wish not to remember you like this every day. But so much of you is in me and so much isn't. I am glad that I do not have to face your constant criticism.

I feel like the forts of Delhi. They stand in their grandeur over years of rain, storm and winds, standing, but stoic in their loneliness.

Love,
Manu

PS: Mahesh called to inform me that Ma ate sweets for lunch and wasted a bowl of rice. She had no appetite. I felt like telling him that depression would eat her up. But I chose to remain mum.

10 March 2023

Bengaluru

Dear Baba,

It is March, and I finally mustered the courage to enter your house. I unlocked the door to your apartment—your place of refuge and freedom. I entered with so much trepidation. I could even hear my heartbeat. The place was quiet and cool. The air in the room was strangely still fresh; the curtains were half drawn. The blue Buddha sculpture basked in its divine light.

There was a thin layer of dust on the furniture. The gas stove was covered with a piece of cloth. There were packets of Kolkata *bori** on the shelves.

I gingerly walked into your bedroom. Time stood still. I could see you on the bed with the remote in hand, watching the Bengali news channels, absolutely angry that the Communist Party of India (Marxist)—the CPI(M)—was out of West Bengal and raging at the Trinamool Congress and Mamata Banerjee. Your sorrow about the Nano project being taken out of Bengal. The helplessness you expressed when you heard about constant government frauds and saw postgraduate students standing in a queue for a job in a hospital's morgue department. Some of the applicants were engineers who needed to earn a living for their families.

I could hear you and Ma amble about in your home.

*It is a form of dried lentil dumplings popular in Bengali cuisine.

It was getting warm. The sunrays from the shut windows lit up the room, drawing patterns. The terracotta goddess you got from Bankura was still there, above your bed on the wall. I looked intently at the art strewn around. I opened the cupboards. Ma's beautiful Bengal silk and cotton saris and matching blouses were on hangers.

It all seemed so unreal. How could life change so much? This cupboard revealed another human being altogether. Now she sits desolate all day in her nightclothes.

As I looked at the bookshelves, I found your hearing aid and a magnifying glass. I held the glass and hoped my debut book would be there among the volumes. I knew you wouldn't keep it in your collection. But I still hoped. Then I gave up looking for it.

Love,
Manu

2 April 2023

Bengaluru

Dear Baba,

You have been gone for over seven months now. It's April, and you are no longer here. I am beginning to acknowledge that you won't ever be around anymore. I can't touch or see you, but I can feel your essence. The only communication I can have with you is via my soul, where you reside, gentler and more communicative than when you were alive.

What amazes me is the beauty of the human nature. It is truly so resilient. As the days pass, I realize that, as a single child, I hardly have anyone to fall back on. I must have my own back, as my strongest and most dependable ally. I am becoming stoic and have slowly started to enjoy my own company. I wish I could not see through things and lies. It doesn't help to be a resilient woman—she is unlovable. A woman finds it easier to be loved if she is demure and weak. Affection is easily bestowed on someone who sees it as a reward and not something that she truly deserves.

I feel many times that it is better to be dull. It's better to be someone who is incapable of questioning the inequalities and dysfunctional realities around her. I learn as I go along that I must try not to question arbitrary behaviour. I know I suffer because I question. Everyone around me is happy and easy as long as I toe the line. But now the time has come and I can no longer be this way—wanting to please everyone and overlooking my emotional needs.

So I have started to cut ties, accept disappointments for what they are and understand that I won't have control over other people's actions towards me. I have also learnt that only our closest people hurt us—because we allow ourselves to open our souls and be vulnerable near them. That's why they have the power to hurt us. When we are hurt, we cannot think straight and feel the world around us is crumbling. But actually, it is the other way around—a new world is being built, and that is what most of us fail to see. The truth is you were healed with death.

I found this out so late. I now view my own growth as stemming from the traumas I endured. I also believe in seeing the good in people I meet. So many have come forward to help me in my life's new journey. I had to learn to trust strangers so that I could open up to them, to receive the universe's magical miracles and gifts.

But there is something that I still struggle with—and that is how you and Ma betrayed me by not supporting my decision to end my marriage.

I thought that being well-read and having travelled across the world, you would understand my trauma. It shocked me that you both wanted me to carry on. I am learning to accept that sometimes parental love isn't what we think it is. It has its limitations. So I am trying to forget the days I wept copiously and neither of you was willing to wipe my tears, hold my hand or tell me not to fear loneliness.

With so much that happened to me, the two magical words that stay are resilience and endurance. These are qualities often overlooked. People who endure hardships sometimes become spiritual or bitter and suspicious of the people around them. But betrayals bring about an internal leap within the self.

It's important to talk about post-trauma growth. This sort of growth is permanent, humbling and beautiful.

It's important to talk about marriage, of women who have survived bad marriages, men who have been respectful towards their wives but who may not have understood their desires. Marriages like yours, that have lasted decades of arguments, companionship, with commitment. The truth is that a marriage isn't an ideal situation for women, who are so often treated like a man's property. Marriages are celebrated so that life won't be empty, but they are mostly empty. Couples after years sleep on the same bed with their backs to each other. Many don't share bedrooms. They learn to disdainfully survive this social construct irrespective of how they feel. Most learn to adjust.

For me, the small hurts leave an indelible impression. One can overlook the bigger storms over time, but the small things said or unsaid, stay forever as bitter memories.

I recall the time when you wanted to start a business. I was barely five maybe and you needed money.

Ma was angry with all your impractical decisions. She took a wad of notes and threw it on the floor for you to pick up. I recall the humiliation and the fights. Even towards your last days, you talked about those incidents. Till the time you could speak, you lamented that no one loved you. But no one asked you—and you never asked yourself—if you loved anyone with respect and kindness.

Hurt remains like injury scabs; one doesn't know when a scab falls off. Suddenly it vanishes. But a deep gash is invisible to the naked eye.

I wish to grow spiritually and realize that we are just a speck in the cosmos we inhabit. If the cosmos wants, it can consume us all like a black hole that consumes all matter. We will enter it, while paying our EMIs and medical bills, managing our disappointments and traumas.

Here is hoping that Ma will let you go, that she will be gentle with herself. And here's hoping that I, in turn, will not get exasperated with her constant need for attention.

Suddenly she said to me today, 'Listen, I want to donate your Baba's Bengali books to a library.'

I was angry that she couldn't understand that when I went to your locked apartment, I soaked myself in the beautiful calligraphy of the Bengali script that drew me close to my being.

Irritated I asked, 'Why?'

She looked with defeat and defiance. Like a tiger would have looked if the calf it was pursuing ran past it. Ma lowered her voice and said, 'No reason, nothing!'

I calmed down and reminded myself to be kinder.

I looked away, and said, 'Okay, we will look for a library.'

We are both lost in our defeated world.

Love you,
Manu

20 May 2023

Bengaluru

Dear Baba,

It's a Saturday and as I wind down for the day, I realize there is not a single person in Bengaluru I can meet at will. Everything needs prep time here. There are no spontaneous friendships in my life here. So to overcome my feelings, I ate a bowl of Maggi and an ice cream.

Is this what is called the displacement effect? That one loses connection with the self in pursuit of bigger material gains? Moving to a new city opens you up in ways that are marvellous and closes you, too, in myriad ways. So one is quick to learn and even quicker to unlearn. I have unlearnt everything that was spontaneous in me.

Ma's talk of displacement makes my anxiety shoot up. She sits in front of me with her face in her hands, looking like a petulant child whose toys have been taken away. She says, 'I miss Delhi. My people and the community living.'

I nod, and my mind travels back to those big homes in South Delhi where the rich people reside, to when I imagined, in my innocence, what a great life they led. I used to be in awe at the thought that they could eat anything they wanted. But I now see life differently. It is now that I miss the community life of our R.K. Puram home. I understand her misery. For Ma, there was always a neighbour coming in or stepping out. A door being open or shut, a smile, a nod, or sometimes just a look—that was

Delhi. She craves that human contact.

I often wish I was simpler. If I were less travelled and exposed, I would have found it easier to fit in. Why do I struggle so much to conform? Is it because grief has eaten my innards and opened up my symbolic third eye? This eye can see more than what others can. With this third eye, I see people's posturing, lies and deceit. Nothing interests me anymore.

I hope this passes. This disinterest is self-destructive. I overeat to rein my heart in.

Love,
Manu

21 March 2023

Bengaluru

Dear Baba,

Haggling with the plumber and pressing him to fix a leaking pipe at home is the same as asking an MBA graduate to work on a business plan. The goal is identical—it is all about getting the job not just done, but done well.

As an ex-housewife and now an entrepreneur, I use the same negotiation skills. The stay-at-home period helped me acquire life skills early on. Of course, there are many steps to this. First is the validation of a decision a housewife makes. It is like presenting the idea to a roundtable of experts who will decide your brain's worth. In many families, the mother-in-law or the father-in-law has the final say, and you learn to deal with the system.

To get the housewife's ideas passed, she has to upgrade her skills from time to time. Sometimes she is the avatar of a hustler, sometimes she tries the soft punch approach, based on a given challenge or situation.

As women grow into this role, they learn to detach their emotions from the decisions they make.

They lower their tone, or raise it, based on the requirements. This is practised across the board of stakeholders.

Management is the key to success. For the housewife, it is practised with the vegetable seller, the house help, plumber, electrician, in-laws, husband and children; for the office-goer, with the HR (Human Resources) or the CFO (chief financial officer) or CEO.

As a novice entrepreneur, I am managing people on an everyday basis. I have been an entrepreneur for four years now, and I still feel like I am walking on thin ice or find myself sinking into the deep end of the ocean. There are rare times when I bask in the endorsement of a happy client. But more often I find myself bawling at the constant insecurities of a bootstrapped entrepreneur.

Two years into writing and podcasting, I was looking at all the challenges the fields posed—I was cheated out of large sums of money and lost faith in people I thought were on the same page as me. Sometimes I dodge, and occasionally, I take the bullet head-on. I recently hired a confident young executive. The scope of work promised was perfect. Money was negotiated and the profit share was included. I employed her with the hope of building a stronger business.

I was relieved that I had finally found the genie. There was a spring in my step.

For the first month, we held lengthy discussions over calls; the industry reports shared were impressive. But I got tired of opening attachments; reading those lengthy reports was out of the question.

To my horror, I found myself nodding to all her suggestions. I thought they were very impressive. I kept reminding myself, 'I don't know the ropes yet.' However, the ideas were only at the ideation level. Nothing concrete was happening.

Soon I found that I was doing all the work. I was

stressing out about finding the vendors for design and guests for my podcast.

Three months into the contract, I requested a review. I said, 'Please send me a report of what we have achieved so far.'

There was silence at the other end. I heard a 'Hmm.' She called and said she had realized she was not the right fit for the JD. JD, I thought. Joint development? I quickly figured that she meant 'job description'.

I do acknowledge that the landscape of work has shifted. It is all digital now, and the new generation is mostly comfortable with Zoom and Google Meet. I couldn't help but reflect on the start of my career. I was obedient, almost servile, which I think was terrible.

Which side is better? It's debatable. There was a time when people were conscientious, accountable and scared to lose their reputation, which was treasured as equity. Reputation is not much of an equity to be treasured any more.

But what happens to entrepreneurs like us who build their businesses on the strength of their reputation at work? In the creative arts business, our investments surpass the returns. Amid all this stress, the pain point as an entrepreneur remains—can I put my trust in someone again at work?

Love,
Manu

22 May 2023

Bengaluru

Dear Baba,

I have just finished an entire week of scripting, writing, and connecting with new people—and I am amazed at the number of good people I have met.

The truth is we actually meet more good than bad. But we have an annoying habit of concentrating more on the bad experiences instead of the good ones.

I often find myself ruminating over the nasty ones. I recall with clarity the teacher who made me feel small for failing maths; I recollect the autoimmune illness that got me bedridden for six months or more; I remember the lonely hours when so-called friends deserted me for not being a part of the party crowd, as the illness took over my life like a gnawing giant, gorging on my spirit and body.

But I gave a good fight. And finally, the pain was gone.

Why is it so easy to forget the schoolteacher who told me to write, paint and dream? The one who put her hand on my head as I struggled with geometry?

I think we selfish human beings take friendships that have lasted decades for granted and keep going back to the ones that didn't last. We have this annoying habit of not feeling grateful enough.

Every day, I must repeat to myself that life is good, bad and ugly, too.

Wisdom is having gratitude for the good and reverence for the bad.

After all, bad experiences are our greatest teachers.

Love,
Manu

23 September 2022

Bengaluru

Dear Baba,

I am much like you, but different. I live in my own little world. After marriage, we had to move to a new city and with it, my own personality shifted. I have lost the idea of friendship. Why do I find it so tough to connect?

The truth is that some friends drain us. I have reinvented myself, and that doesn't sit well with many.

I keep telling myself that I need to be calmer, deeper and kinder. But the truth is I feel lonely and have maybe only two good friends in my life.

There is not much emotional openness in many of the people I meet. To truly connect one needs to be able to open up and be willing to share concerns and issues. But friendship is sometimes so superficial, and mostly about just meeting for a drink. No one cares beyond the weekend plans.

I am desperate to find someone with whom I can share deep emotions and yet be silly.

We need different things for our different sides. As much as I crave someone who is intelligent and warm, I need that hug from a tightly-knit circle too. And a laugh with people with whom you can be yourself.

I never knew that over time, friends would be a serious minority in my life.

Most say that your spouse becomes a friend over the years. But what happens when the long-time partner is fearful and wants to hold you back from finding your feet?

Most find it easy to hold on to my older self. I want to tell them that the old me is dead. And to tell them not to be threatened by my new version. It can only get better. I long for honest and good friendships, but I am a loner, too. People irritate me with their texts of positivity. Sadness isn't a crime.

These days I suffer from insomnia. My mind wants me to listen to it. It's been trying to tell me to embrace this change and accept that change means a shift from the past. So naturally, the old equations die their own death. I need to accept that.

With you gone, I am free from your condemnation and disapproval of me. I don't know why I thought of you as my audience. Honestly, you didn't care about my reboot or even bothered about it. What mattered was whether I shared my car with you for your errands, or went to the doctor for your check-ups. The rest didn't matter. I am learning to accept that my journey is a solo one and I will grow with my roots ensconced in the deep earth, embellished with golden fruits and silver stars. The only one watching over me is the universe, helping me manifest my goals by gently holding my finger. It is helping me jump over the deep pond of sarcasm into the sunlight that bathes my body.

Love,
Manu

24 May 2023

Bengaluru

Dear Baba,

I just received an invite to give a talk about reinventing my life to a few women of Bengaluru. I am always nervous about speaking in public. How do I open up my heart to people who will brave the city's mad traffic to listen to me? Will I do justice, will I be honest enough and hope my story will touch them in some way?

Should I tell them the truth that none of you wanted me to reboot? Starting work meant I would be unavailable to you all. It would also mean a more powerful me. This was definitely not the ideal Mohua you all had got used to. Neel was the only one who said, 'Don't give up.'

You all would have wanted me to be powerless, scrounging for money, with oodles of time in hand to deal with each of your childish demands. And yes, to have me around at all times—running to hospitals, being the caregiver, the pet nurturer. All this, with not a pat on my back. The idea was to push me forever, hoping I would continue without questioning, and never wake up from this slumber!

I suppose household chores are a great way to trap a woman. Just burden her with quotes on the selflessness and virtues of being an obedient mother, wife and daughter. So women follow the script.

I carried on for years, too—managing a home and

enabling an environment where everyone and everything was taken care of. I had to manage the staff at home, too. When someone didn't want another child, I would take them to the hospital. Some got married and I was again helping them set up their lives. I invested my years and my emotions to run this home like a well-oiled machine. So yes, it would have inconvenienced you all if I started working.

It is truly difficult for women to be independent. Economic independence is power and no one wants to shake the house of cards. One gust of wind, and the queen might go right up, toppling the others. Who wants a powerful queen? The answer is—no one. A woman is often given credit for her beauty and righteousness, but very rarely for her intelligence. I wrote my first book, *Nautanki Saala and Other Stories*, and you didn't even open its first page. None of you, barring Neel, read or discussed my book. You made me feel that 'I was not enough!'

But I know I am enough and will finally write with my bleeding heart. The readers may be strangers but they all belong to this narrative, in one way or another.

Love,
Manu

25 December 2022

Bengaluru

Dear Baba,

Love is fleeting. It arrives in bursts and leaves one in the throes of destruction. It is like a drug that boosts your immunity—to leave you sickly again. Only a few are lucky enough to experience a spiritual awakening through love. Love, for most, is like how a child gets hooked to the sweet stickiness of the mother's milk, wanting more and more of the life-saving nectar. But eventually, the mother's milk dries up, leaving the child lost in resentment, just like most people in love.

Love is also that lost poem that flutters away, like the faded prayer flags hanging on a Buddhist monastery. The multicoloured little fragments of cloth, standing against the mountain winds while becoming withered. Love, I guess, is for the brave. Or for the lucky ones.

Ma has opened her album with photographs of the two of you—young, healthy and good-looking. The beautiful photo of you stealing a glance at Ma, who has her eyes lowered like a coy bride with a garland in her hand. I also found a photo where Ma has stuck your photo with hers. Must have been the days when you both were seeing each other. The photo, in particular, is bursting with the seamlessness of a shared culture—love for reading and wanting to start a beautiful life together. You don't know, in that picture, that Ma would have only one child, a daughter, and the other one would bleed to death in her first trimester. I must admit I never saw myself with a brother or a sister. So I didn't feel anything when I was told I would never have a sibling.

I had seen your love for Ma. You were angry with me all the time when she was so sick. As if it was my fault that I was alive. I recall once I finished all the butter that I used to smear on those thin arrowroot biscuits, it angered you. You were so angry all the time.

In my little heart, I questioned many times if I was really born out of you both.

I do remember you taking me to Nazareth Hospital in Shillong to see Ma. I didn't comprehend the intensity of the situation. I remember walking the hilly roads with your hand in mine. I was floating in the aroma of the bakeries on the way to the hospital, with their freshly baked biscuits, the jam and butter concoctions. The Shillong sun was setting. The chapel looked forlorn yet strikingly beautiful. The roads were small, and the occasional buses passed us by. We walked along the roads together. I wanted to pluck the flowers growing out of the moss-filled walls of the hilly roads. But I didn't want to anger you. So I walked quietly, stealing a glance here and there.

Ma was in hospital for almost a month. Our home suddenly had relatives. They took over the kitchen, which was messy and unclean. I remember your aunt sitting on the cold, clammy floor. She used to sit there to cut vegetables and cook. But what stays most is that she left her home to look after ours. The relatives reprimanded you gently, 'Chandan, don't be harsh on Manu.' But you were angry and nervous. I understand that only now.

You had nearly lost your Moni, as you lovingly called her. Your world seemed to fall apart. But finally, Ma's health was restored and life got back into its normal groove. However, the fear of angering you or Ma stayed on.

I remember the sterile environment of the hospital. Ma sat on the hospital bed in a gown, her long hair touching her hips. She smiled at me. I could barely reach her. I told her to come home soon as you were so angry with me for having finished the butter.

The years passed by. None of us touches butter any more. But where did the love vanish? Or was there love that I somehow missed?

Maybe love was in the little things you did for each other. She would make coconut fritters for you, deep fried, with dry red chillies, and you would buy her favourite dosa breakfast. I guess the only way you could deal with loneliness was by eating. Food gives you a feeling of happiness for a few hours. I relate to that. I do this often, too—drown myself in food. The chain of memories pushes me into an abyss of emptiness.

It's like the dried nipples of the mother's breast. The child still searches for milk and will suckle any nipple they find milk in. All they need is the reassurance of being full and safe. Like life in love, there is death in love too. Here it is like the corpse of a mother, cold, still, unmoving, yet with the debris of the past promise of warm milk oozing out of her body.

After years of togetherness, I found that you both reconnected when it came to my child, for his school and college achievements. The food you both cooked and the home you both ran. But love between you two was also like a sliver of light in the darkness that covered you both. Yet in that togetherness was the undying spirit of a nature that was independent, fierce and feisty. There was anger brimming like a vessel bubbling with a lid. It is on the stove and promises to overflow if you don't take off the lid and put out the fire underneath.

Your marriage was like most marriages—underlying hurt and grief, individual dreams that were thwarted, the pressure of raising children; outwardly, looking happy and content. So unhappy, yet also happy in bits and pieces.

I think marriage is almost like a cage, where tamed animals fit in because their parents fit in. It's a chain that can't be broken. Patriarchy is robbing marriage of its love. No wonder many are opting to stay single nowadays.

My marriage wasn't easy. I feel I let myself down and was bitterly let down, too. I look back at the promises I had made with life. And how ego and again the slur of *dkhar*, an outsider, came to play its role in my life. I was rebellious and didn't marry a Bengali Brahmin boy as Ma would've wanted. I must admit, I do feel I may have missed the beautiful innocent traditions, such as *gaye holud* and the couple trying to find a cowrie within a bowl of milk. It was totally different for me from the start.

It hurt that my in-laws couldn't accept a Bengali bride. Slowly, the love faded. I couldn't see myself toeing the line forever, as there was always a rebel in me. I found it difficult then to understand the parochial nature of smaller communities that tried to hold on to a dying culture, that felt threatened by the existence of other cultures beyond their own.

It is only now that I understand that there may be some truth in holding on to a place we call home. Home is where the broth is familiar, a concoction of age-old ways passed on through generations. So there may be some truth in love lasting in such spaces of familiarity.

Or perhaps all couples face this, irrespective of the commonalities? Love is supposed to be found, lost, and found again. The dejections and rejections, and the inability to start all over again make couples stay on. It eventually becomes a habit. One can't do without the other. Like you both.

It is in the toxicity, and in the tremendous acts of kindness amidst all this, that love survives—like a sapling that breaks out of parched land. The sapling stands stoic and looks up to the sun, notwithstanding the shifting earth, the torrential rains and the harsh winds.

Have you seen such a sapling? It looks benevolent, drenched in drops of gold, just like a prayer that has been answered. It tells us we'd rather love and lose than never have loved and lost.

The joy is in finding a path in that loss. And finding light, like the sapling.

My fingers are getting numb and I must grab a coffee before I come back to you again.

Were you deeply in love with Ma? According to me, you loved and hated in equal measure.

It's just that your cup for me was mostly empty. But without this emptiness, I would never have found the writer in me.

I need my coffee now. I need to hold the cup and feel its warmth, encircle it in my hands, hug it for the high it gives me when so much else is a downer.

I miss you.

Love,
Manu

HOPE

1 June 2023

Bengaluru

Dear Baba,

I have come full circle with my life, at least in some parts.

I have had so many eminent guests on my podcast. Most said they enjoyed talking to me. The criticism from you and a few others is slowly wearing off. It was like a large, dried-up scab. It has been breaking away, inch by inch. I can finally feel the air on the skin below the scab. I feel free.

I recently interviewed Ila Arun. Her voice was raspy, yet sweet and full of emotion.

I watched her play yesterday at the city's finest theatre space, Ranga Shankara. The play was an adaptation of Henrik Ibsen's *Ghosts*. It was set in India, around a haveli in Rajasthan where the debauchery of the royalty was portrayed. Ila Arun was the queen widow, who lived in a large palace but amid all its wealth, led a life filled with grief, anger and despair. Her husband used to be a womanizer who didn't spare anyone. Ila did a great job in essaying the role of the queen.

The play made me think of our generational wounds. I worry so much about my child. I hope he will not carry our curse of being so emotional that even the smallest trigger can cause an avalanche of unresolved, pent-up grief. I hope my son is blessed with good people around him.

Love,
Manu

2 June 2023

Bengaluru

Dear Baba,

I miss the long letters we wrote each other when you travelled, which was often. Those envelopes that the postman delivered had pages and pages of information about the books that you were reading or had read. They were inspiring for my young mind, which was full of awe and hope.

I yearn to receive a handwritten note now. The last one I received was an apology letter from Chini.

Those long letters I received from you during my school and college days had glimpses of your thoughts. They were powerful, hopeful and full of revolutionary ideas. They were full of stories about the architects of nations, about wars, inventions, art, music, theatre and political upheavals.

In one such letter, you wrote, 'Have you started smoking?'

It had made me smile. I replied to you, 'I like the idea of these very intellectual women smoking, reciting *nazms*[*], so cool in their demeanour. But I start choking on smoke, so I doubt I will ever learn to look cool smoking. There has to be another method of mastering this persona.'

---

[*]It is a form of Urdu poetry, a generic term for non-ghazal poetry that came to Urdu under the influence of English poetry during the second half of the 20th century, and soon established its independent presence.

I mentioned this to my college friends, who were all girls. They were aghast and couldn't understand how a father could ask his daughter this question. Most led quite a restricted life and were not open with their parents. Many were busy studying or learning to cook better than their mothers. I took no interest in cooking. But I do think now that cooking is meditative and a great art form.

Among all the letters, I especially remember the one you wrote to me about the Wright brothers. It was perhaps ten pages long.

Those were the days of handwritten letters with ink-filled pens. Your beautiful, almost calligraphic, lettering beckoned from the lined sheets. I felt so happy when I received those thick envelopes with your letters. I took the time to read and reread each page.

This particular letter was about the marvel of the invention of the aeroplane. The Wright brothers' perseverance impressed me. So I think I took a bit out of their bower of thoughts—to continue, to resist and fly on, unperturbed.

The Wright brothers became famous in the United States and worldwide as they took their first flight in the machine in North Carolina. They piloted and flew their heavier-than-air machine on the morning of 17 December 1903. You wrote these lines and I could see your face telling me with delight about inventions and discoveries. About the madness in the genius.

The brothers did not know what they were doing for posterity. Wilbur and Orville Wright were creating a mass weapon of war for history to remember.

The invention also strengthened class divisions among

people around the world. The rich could fly and the poor used the road and railways. Things have changed a bit now; many people fly, cutting across strata. I have inherited some of your genes. I feel happy when I see people from smaller towns taking a flight to reach a place for medical treatment or for a holiday. It shows the growth of a nation, from one perspective.

The division, however, is still there—we have business class, first class and economy or 'cattle' class in planes. Then there are the private jets.

But I have to admit the enormous benefits of this invention. Time is saved and travel has become easier for people. It is a boon—but only if utilized for good purposes, which is such a stupid utopian thought.

The reality is that we are surrounded by a dysfunctional and dystopian society that thrives on finishing tribal cultures, old systems, forests and fields. What happens if Shillong sets up an airport? Think of the acres of forest that will be destroyed.

I wish I could receive such letters from you. Each letter is clear, with words neatly arranged in rows. Those neat and clean lines that were so mesmerizing to read.

Love,
Manu

4 June 2023

Bengaluru

Dear Baba,

Do you remember how, in the dialysis centre, you kept telling me not to give up on my marriage, which had actually ended a long time earlier? I kept quiet. Exasperated, you looked away. Why did you and Ma want me to stay on unhappily in an arrangement that wasn't working?

I feel free to be able to work. I don't need to deal with the meanness of his cousins or deal with constant humiliation and disrespect.

I do worry for myself. My future looks uncertain, with no one there for me in the city. But at this juncture, I don't know what matters.

Would staying back in the marriage make me strong, and does breaking off make me a failure? I read an article where an author lauded couples who stuck it out despite differences. It irked me. Why should two unhappy people, who may have got over the physical memory of sex, stay together? Why should two jaded people hold on to their marriage because the wife's social identity is linked to the husband's?

As a housewife, I had no other identity—apart from being the mother of my child, wife to my husband, daughter-in-law, sister-in-law, and other such equations. I was never a person on my own.

Yes, it was scary to sever the identity. But, you know, I

have watched the sad gaze of many lost housewives, buried beneath a pile of utensils, unkempt clothes and leftover emotions of detection and rejections.

If you looked closer, you would see this contradiction of wanting to belong to this comfort zone, yet wanting to break out of the cage.

Most women can no longer express what they want from life. What a woman expresses in her timidity, instead, is the resignation of a life snuffed out when the flame had just begun blazing with a passion for the self.

I refused to stay frightened forever. This didn't sit well with you and Ma. But I just had to do what I felt was right. And I'm ready to face what life brings to me. This time, on my own terms.

Neel is okay, and nothing matters more than that.

Love,
Manu

6 June 2023

Bengaluru

Dear Baba,

I don't think I can quite end writing letters to you. But it has to end. My search for myself as seen from your eyes has to end, and I have to bid you farewell.

So much has changed for me since you left in August 2022.

Your home remains locked as it's difficult for me to open the rooms. I can see you and find you in the little and large ways of the house. The shelf of Bengali books. The magnifying glass to read the small print. The bed with one of Neel's baby blue cushions. The terracotta Ma Durga on the wall above the window. The bathroom. Your denture bowl. So much is there.

You will live forever in my love for travel, books, cinema, food and also in my straightforwardness. I will remain like you, with my unvanquished dream of a place I can call home. You searched for it till you lived and so will I. We are fated to be alike.

I sincerely hope you have found peace in death. If we are to believe in Hindu tenets, you have been reborn somewhere. I hope this time you have been born in Florence. Maybe I will find the same glint in a little boy's eyes when I travel there. Just around the museum, a place where they have the best art in the world, you may be basking in the sun.

Maybe I will recognize you and you will tell me about

Dante. And if our souls recognize each other, let's hug and make up and say I love you, without feeling embarrassed or shy.

You are alive every day with me. I find you in the butterflies that flit around me. I find you when the clouds move around in an azure sky. It is in the small things I see your gnarled, wrinkled hands, pointing me in a direction that I may not have taken otherwise.

Love,
Manu

10 June 2023

Bengaluru

Dear Baba,

I end our written conversation here. There is always so much to say, and I realize it's endless. I have learnt so much from you. And unlearnt, too.

Now I must learn to let go of pretence. Those forced smiles, the hidden tears and the expressed anger, too, must stop. I am not going to worry any longer about what people think of me.

I only pray that I have more and more gratitude for the life I have led so far. I am looking forward to my days of writing. Your love for books and the way you described situations will remain my compass, guiding me ahead.

I believe writing enlightens us in ways unimaginable. Unknown feelings get addressed and words heal as the wounds close with words.

I do think that the *Brahman* in Hinduism, referred to as knowledge, is present in each one of us. It remains unseen, unfelt and unknown even to those who gain the required knowledge. The ones who think they recognize that seat of knowledge are actually far away from self-actualization.

Our ego comes in the way, stopping us from surrendering to the divine—the light that can't be found but resides in each of us.

From hereon I will no longer—at least will try not to—cling to myself, the memory of you, within me via my letters to you. I will not waste my energy to control all that is not meant for me. Or force things to work towards my selfish needs. I will try, with earnestness, I promise you.

I have learnt that the more power you give away, the more it comes back to you. The power that you had over me with your words said and unsaid.

It's the way forward in life for me.

I know, too, that we are all in a state of constant death. We just don't realize it. We hold on to something so tight that it chokes us. The truth is that we are all dissolving. Everything is in decay. It's time for me to accept this transience.

I have tried to let go of my hurt by writing letters to you. I realize now that there is actually nothing to let go of. It eventually has to go. Everything will vanish, leaving not a trace behind. You have vanished into an unreachable realm.

Finally, Baba, you were a great father. You gave me the power of education and sense. You were the greatest grandfather ever to Neel. You tried very hard to make things happen for your family. I stay eternally grateful for the books at home, the music, the sensory awareness of food and smell and the nostalgia attached to memory. It is beautiful and vast like the ocean. It calms me in times of anguish.

You will live forever, in my fingers, my chin, my forehead and my affinity for some things that you passed on. Just like the shiuli blossom that blooms, come what may, during Pujo.

Durga Pujo won't ever be the same, though, for you won't be around. But the fragrance of the flowers will remain in my heart, invigorating my senses. The *godhuli bela*[*] of every Pujo will stay entrenched in my heart, as I travel to Karol Bagh in Delhi, as a 15-year-old girl, buying new clothes and having a cold coffee with you.

Nothing has changed, yet so much has.

I know that I will find you everywhere. You will surprise me with a waft of a cool breeze on a hot summer afternoon; you will be somewhere around during a coffee and cake in a café, as the butterfly that will emerge on the glass pane, fluttering its wings against the light.

I promise not to run after the butterfly. I promise to sit soundlessly and watch it dance around me. It will remind me of a place called home which will forever be with you, Ma and Neel.

Love,
Manu

[*]Literally, the dust raised by the cows returning to their sheds during dusk.

Acknowledgements

A big thank you to my editor, Bishaka Dey Sarkar, without whom this extremely personal piece of writing would not have been possible.

And love to my son, Neel Mandana, whose presence in my life and support keeps me alive.